LAUGHING AT NULL

A HUMOROUS GUIDE TO SOFTWARE LIFE

2023 © Mabrouk Mahdhi

Senior Technical Consultant
contact@mahdhi.com

———————

Cover photo by @cookie_studio on Freepik

To my loving mother *Zina*,

Thank you for being the anchor in my life, providing unwavering support, and nurturing me with your boundless love. Your presence is a source of comfort and strength, and I am eternally grateful for the joy and warmth you bring to every moment we share.

...

To my dearest father *Nacer Kohila*,

In the pages of this book, I find solace and strength, knowing that you have been with me every step of the way. Your unwavering love, guidance, and wisdom have shaped the person I am today, both as a coder and as a human being.

Though you may not physically be here with me anymore, your spirit lives on in the lines of code I write, in the algorithms I craft, and in the passion I carry for the world of technology that we both cherished. You were my first teacher, my biggest supporter, and my greatest inspiration.

With all my love and gratitude,

MABROUK

Roses are red,
Violets are blue:
Always test your code,
before it tests you..

— HASSAN HABIB

Foreword

Dear Readers,

I had the privilege of being one of the first to read this book by Mabrouk Mahdhi and I am happy to write a short foreword for you.

Mabrouk is an experienced and passionate software developer who has been working in various industries and projects for over a decade. He has gained a lot of experience in the field of software engineering.

In this book, Mabrouk takes you on an entertaining and educational journey through the world of software development. He shows you how to master the challenges, joys, and curiosities of this exciting profession. He uses humorous analogies, stories, and examples to make the complex concepts and processes understandable and accessible.

The goal of this book is to give you not only the knowledge and skills you need to deliver successful software projects, but also the attitude and perspective you need to get the most out of your work. Mabrouk wants to show you how to achieve your software development goals with humor, creativity, and passion.

I am impressed with the work and dedication that Mabrouk has put into this book. He has shared not only his extensive knowledge and experience, but also his personality and humor. He has written a book that is both informative and inspiring.

I am sure you will enjoy and benefit from this book, whether you are an experienced software developer, a beginner, or just a curious reader. I invite you to let Mabrouk take you into the fascinating world of software development. *Let's laugh at NULL together!*

— ANDRÉ DAMMEYER

Preface

The world of software engineering: where our days oscillate between the euphoria of solving a problem and the depths of despair when faced with a new one (often of our own making). Where null isn't just an absence of value but a looming specter that's haunted many a late-night coding session. Where the phrase "It works on my machine" is both a defense and a cry for help.

Welcome to "Laughing at Null: A Humorous Guide to Software Life".

Writing this book was a journey of nostalgia. I ventured into the alleys of memory, recalling every quirky incident, every infuriating bug, and every triumphant deployment. This book is not just a reflection of the software engineering life; it's a collection of tales, lessons, and, most importantly, laughs from the myriad experiences many of us share.

Why humor, you ask? Well, if you've ever tried explaining to a non-developer the tragicomedy of a misplaced semicolon or the existential dread of an unexpected null, you'll understand. Humor, I believe, is our collective coping mechanism. It's the light that illuminates the often perplexing, always fascinating labyrinth of code we navigate daily.

Beyond the intricate lines of code and the daunting jargon, I wanted to craft a narrative that speaks to everyone - not just those with a tech-savvy brain. *And what better way to do this than with characters that have made us laugh, ponder, and sometimes even shout at our TV screens?* By reimagining Mr. Bean, Tom, and Jerry as software engineers, we transpose their universal, comedic appeal into the intricate world of software development.

Mr. Bean, with his bumbling yet creative approach, exemplifies the unpredictable nature of coding. Tom & Jerry, with their perpetual game of one-upmanship, reflect the continual back-and-forth we experience as developers. By placing these characters in a software setting, we're bridging the gap between complex technical concepts and relatable, everyday scenarios.

Why is this narrative approach? Because the world of software isn't confined to just techies. In today's digital age, everyone – from young students to our grandparents – interacts with technology daily. By making software engineering narratives more engaging and accessible, we empower a broader audience to peek behind the curtain. This book aims not just to educate but also to demystify, ensuring that tech topics are not an arcane domain but an open book (pun intended) for anyone with a spark of curiosity. Through humor, and our beloved personages, complex topics unfurl into tales of adventure, challenge, and triumph.

Throughout these pages, you'll find the Software Development Life Cycle (SDLC) reimagined as a sitcom, coding analogized with conversing with toddlers, and insights into why version control might just be the closest thing we have to a time machine. This book is for every software engineer who's ever needed a laugh amidst lines of code, for every student looking for camaraderie in compilers, and for anyone curious about the funny bones that support the skeleton of software development.

As you flip through these chapters, I hope you find solace in shared experiences, joy in the idiosyncrasies of our profession, and perhaps even a chuckle or two that eases a rough coding day. Because, in the end, while null might be an absence in code, our collective laughter ensures it never defines our spirit.

— MABROUK MAHDHI

Contents

1

The Software Development Life Cycle (SDLC) as a Sitcom

In the exhilarating sitcom of software development, every day is a new episode, filled with unexpected plot twists, comedic blunders, and moments of pure genius. In this chapter, we take you on a guided tour through the Software Development Life Cycle (SDLC), with each stage set as a memorable sitcom scene. Strap in for a humorous journey, where the laughs are plentiful, and the lessons are invaluable!

1 Planning: Let's Guess the Future

If you've ever planned a trip, a surprise party, or even just a dinner out, you understand that good planning is often the key to success.

Plannig in software development, however, is like trying to predict the future with a foggy crystal ball. You make educated guesses, cross your fingers, and hope that the magical world of coding, like in Harry Putter, is in your favor.

1.1   The Essential Role of Planning

As with any journey, our trek into the realm of software development begins with planning. Imagine setting out on a road trip without a map, no knowledge of the destination, the fuel gauge perilously close to 'E', and the small voice in the backseat incessantly asking, *"Are we there yet*?" Sounds like a recipe for disaster, right? This is the chaotic abyss we teeter on the edge of when we neglect planning in software development.

Planning serves as the blueprint for our software project. It guides the process, establishes clear goals, and most importantly, it gives us an answer when that pesky voice (typically a stakeholder) asks, *"Are we there yet?"*

1.2   The Art of Estimation: Balancing Optimism, Pessimism, and Reality

Estimating in software development is an art form—a delicate balance between optimism, pessimism, and the cold, hard reality. We want to believe that we can build Facebook 2.0 in a weekend, but past experience and the ever-ticking clock remind us of our earthly constraints.

Yet, despite the trickiness, estimating time and resources is a cornerstone of planning. Without it, we risk promising the stars only to deliver a handful of moon dust. Remember, under-promising and over-delivering is typically better received than the other way around!

1.3   Decoding the Enigma of 'Requirements'

If planning is the blueprint, requirements are the measurements—it's knowing that you're building a two-bedroom house, not a skyscraper. Yet, 'requirements' in software development are often as elusive as a chameleon in a bag of Skittles.

Sometimes, they're clear-cut; other times, they are as clear as mud. In many cases, requirements evolve, appearing as one thing initially and then metamorphosing as the project progresses. This is perfectly normal, and we can laugh at the inherent unpredictability even as we adapt and revise our plans accordingly.

1.4   Lessons from the Field: Common (and Comedic) Planning Pitfalls

In software development, planning is a critical phase where we lay the foundation for a successful project. However, it's not always a smooth sailing process, and many developers can relate to the experience of looking back at their past projects and finding amusement in the planning mishaps that occurred. These humorous situations are not just moments for laughter, they also hold valuable lessons that can enhance our future planning endeavors.

One common mistake is setting overly optimistic timelines. It's easy to get excited about a new project and underestimate the time required for various tasks. As a result, deadlines can become unrealistic and lead to stress and rushed work towards the end. By reflecting on these instances, we learn the importance of setting realistic and achievable timelines, allowing us to distribute tasks more effectively and avoid unnecessary pressure.

Another pitfall involves what might seem like minor features turning into major endeavors. In software development, even seemingly straightforward additions can have unforeseen complexities that emerge as we dive deeper into the implementation. Recognizing this tendency helps us better analyze and assess potential features before committing to them fully. It's crucial to evaluate the scope of each task and communicate effectively with stakeholders to avoid scope creep and maintain project focus.

The unpredictable nature of software development also teaches us the significance of being adaptable and flexible in our planning. No matter how meticulously we plan, unexpected challenges and requirements will inevitably arise. By acknowledging this reality, we can build resilience into our planning process, enabling us to adjust and pivot when needed.

A sense of humor is an essential tool to navigate the ups and downs of software development. Laughter helps us stay positive and creative when facing challenges, fostering a healthy team environment and boosting morale. Embracing humor in the face of setbacks allows us to learn from mistakes without dwelling on them negatively.

2   Analysis: Playing 20 Questions with Stakeholders

Let's venture into the next phase of our software development sitcom, where we try to decipher the wants, needs, and sometimes baffling requests of stakeholders. Consider this the *"Who's on First?"* of the software world.

2.1 The Essential Role of Effective Communication with Stakeholders

Effective communication with stakeholders is to project success what milk is to cookies. Without it, we're left with a dry, crumbly mess. Yet, despite its importance, communication is often a stumbling block in many projects.

It's not so much the talking part—most of us are pretty good at that—it's the listening and understanding that can get tricky.

Stakeholders are our guides on this wild ride, the ones holding the map *(even if it sometimes feels like it's upside down)*. Properly interpreting their needs and expectations is key to steering the project in the right direction. Further insights on the importance of good communication will be elaborated upon in Chapter 7.

2.2 The Art of Asking the Right Questions

If stakeholder communication is a game of 20 Questions, then asking the right questions is an art. Too general, and you're left scratching your head over vague answers. Too specific, and you risk drowning in unnecessary details.

Our job as software engineers is to extract the useful nuggets of information that will help shape our project, without falling down the rabbit hole of irrelevant specifics. Remember, no question is a bad question if it brings you closer to understanding the project's true requirements.

2.3   Misinterpretations and Their Comical (or Catastrophic) Consequences

Misinterpretations can lead to some funny (or facepalm-inducing) moments. There's nothing quite like the comedy of launching a feature that bears no resemblance to what the stakeholder had in mind, despite the dozens of meetings and countless emails exchanged.

While amusing in retrospect, these miscommunications can also lead to costly delays and rework. They serve as reminders of the importance of clear, concise, and regular communication with stakeholders, and of double (or triple) checking our interpretations.

2.4   Tips for a Productive Analysis Phase

Now that we've laughed at (and learned from) our past mistakes, let's look at some practical tips for a productive analysis phase. Remember to:

- **Listen actively**: Truly engage in the conversation and show that you're not just hearing, but understanding.
- **Ask for clarifications**: If something doesn't make sense, ask for an explanation. It's better to ask now than to regret it later.
- **Recap regularly**: Regularly summarize your understanding of the requirements to ensure you and the stakeholders are on the same page.

As our journey through the sitcom of the SDLC continues, we're heading into the Design phase next, where we'll architect The Empire State Building...with Jenga blocks.

3 Design: Architecting The Empire State Building ... in Jenga Blocks

Onwards we go, from the delightful round of 20 questions to the nail-biting stage of design, where we try to build the Empire State Building using Jenga [1] blocks, all while hoping it won't crumble in the lightest breeze. Strap in for some laughs, gasps, and valuable lessons.

3.1 The Importance of Robust Software Architecture

Picture this: you're tasked with building a skyscraper — a modern marvel that will stand tall amidst its peers. However, the only materials you have at your disposal are Jenga blocks. Sounds daunting, right? *Welcome to the life of a software engineer.*

Designing a robust software architecture is akin to building a skyscraper. Both need a solid foundation, careful planning, and the ability to withstand external forces. Ignore these essentials, and your magnificent structure could very well turn into a pile of rubble (or bug-infested code) before your eyes.

3.2 The Perils of Rushing or Neglecting the Design Phase

In our quest for quick results, it's tempting to rush through or entirely skip the design phase. After all, *who needs a blueprint when you're*

---

[1]   Jenga ® is a registered trademark of Hasbro, Inc. The use of the term 'Jenga' in this book is for illustrative purposes only and should not be construed as an endorsement or affiliation with Hasbro, Inc.

armed with enthusiasm and a box of Jenga blocks?

Well, as anyone who's ever played Jenga will tell you, removing or misplacing just one block can send the whole tower tumbling. The same applies to software design. Overlook one minor detail, and you might find yourself scrambling to pick up the pieces of your crumbled code.

3.3 Funny Anecdotes About Over-complicated or Oversimplified Designs

When it comes to design, there's a thin line between "ingeniously complex" and "unnecessarily complicated," just as there's a delicate balance between "elegantly simple" and "oversimplified." Straying too far in either direction can lead to some comical, forehead-slapping moments. These stories serve as cautionary tales, offering valuable lessons for developers and designers alike.

3.3.1 The Case of the Rube Goldberg Code

Once upon a time, in a software development team not so far away, there was a developer who had a reputation for creating solutions that resembled Rube Goldberg machines [1].

In this particular project, the developer was tasked with designing a simple feature to update user profiles. Instead of a straightforward form, the developer crafted an intricate system that required users to navigate through a series of convoluted menus, press multiple buttons in a specific sequence, and solve a puzzle reminiscent of a Rubik's Cube just to change their email address. The end result

---

[1]   A Rube Goldberg machine is a complex contraption designed to perform a simple task in a convoluted and overly intricate manner.

was both impressive and absurdly complicated.

3.3.2   The One-Button Fiasco

In another corner of the software development world, there was a designer who firmly believed in the mantra "less is more." This designer was determined to simplify the user interface to the extreme, aiming for a single button that would do everything. This button, labeled *"Go,"* was meant to encompass all possible actions within the software.

Users soon found themselves in a comical situation where they had to click the "Go" button to write emails, update their profiles, send messages, and even order pizza. The simplicity of having only one button had led to a lack of clarity, leaving users utterly bewildered about how to accomplish even the most basic tasks.

3.3.3   The Great Back-and-Forth Debate

In a collaborative project involving multiple designers and developers, a heated debate emerged over the placement of a single button. Some argued it should be placed at the top of the screen for easy access, while others insisted it should be at the bottom for better reachability. The debate escalated to the point where a two-week-long discussion ensued, complete with colorful diagrams and impassioned speeches.

In the end, the team implemented a dynamic button that moved between the top and bottom of the screen depending on the user's scrolling behavior. While this solution may have seemed like a brilliant compromise, it led to users chasing the elusive button like a game of whack-a-mole, resulting in endless frustration and, eventually, laughter within the team.

3.3.4 Lessons Learned

These amusing anecdotes serve as reminders that striking the right balance in design is crucial. Overly complicated designs can confuse and frustrate users, while oversimplified ones can lead to absurd and impractical solutions. The key is to find a middle ground that prioritizes usability, functionality, and user experience.

3.4 Tips for Designing Scalable, Maintainable, and Robust Software

Designing software that is scalable, maintainable, and robust is critical for long-term success. It ensures that as the software grows in complexity and usage, it will continue to function optimally and meet the demands of its users. While there are many ways to achieve this, here are some foundational principles to guide you:

(1) **Keep It Simple:** Albert Einstein famously said, "Everything should be made as simple as possible, but not simpler." This adage is particularly true for software design. The simpler your architecture and design, the easier it is to understand, maintain, and scale. Avoid overengineering and focus on building solutions that solve the current problem without introducing unnecessary complexities.

(2) **Modularity:** Break down your software into modular components. This allows each piece to be developed, tested, and scaled independently. When changes are required, they can be made in one module without affecting the entire system. This approach makes the software more maintainable and lessens the chances of unintended side effects.

(3) **Consistent Coding Standards:** Ensure that your team follows consistent coding standards. This aids in making the code

readable and maintainable. When a new developer joins the team or when the codebase grows, consistent code can reduce the learning curve and improve collaboration.

(4) **Stateless Design:** Whenever possible, design your applications to be stateless. Stateless systems are easier to scale horizontally because any server can handle any request without requiring knowledge about prior interactions.

(5) **Opt for Scalable Technologies:** Choose technologies and platforms that are known for their scalability. Databases, for instance, should be chosen based on how well they scale, handle concurrency, and manage large datasets.

(6) **Plan for Failures:** Every system will face issues. Plan for them. Implement fail-safes, backup procedures, and redundancy. Design your software so it can handle failures gracefully without causing widespread disruption.

(7) **Frequent Iteration and Feedback:** Regularly review and iterate your design based on feedback from stakeholders, users, and performance metrics. This continuous improvement approach ensures that the software evolves in the right direction and can adapt to changing requirements.

(8) **Documentation:** Maintain up-to-date documentation. This includes architectural diagrams, API specifications, and explanations of core algorithms and decisions. A well-documented system helps onboard new developers and facilitates maintenance as the software evolves.

(9) **Performance Testing:** Regularly conduct performance and stress tests to identify bottlenecks and optimize your software. Understand the limits of your system and design it to handle peak loads efficiently.

(10) **Consider Future Growth:** While you shouldn't overengineer,

it's crucial to anticipate areas where growth might occur. This could be in the form of increased user numbers, more extensive data processing, or the addition of new features. Design with some level of flexibility to accommodate these potential future requirements.

In conclusion, designing scalable, maintainable, and robust software requires a balanced approach of simplicity, foresight, and adaptability. By keeping Einstein's words in mind and ensuring simplicity at the heart of your design, you'll set the stage for a system that can gracefully evolve and stand the test of time.

4 Development: Writing the World's Most Complex Novel

Just as we're dusting off the debris from our Jenga architecture, we find ourselves faced with another monumental task. It's time to pen down the most complex novel ever written — in binary. Welcome to the world of development, where we turn our wild dreams and meticulous designs into tangible reality. Hold onto your keyboards; it's going to be quite a ride.

4.1 The Process of Transforming Design into Reality

There's a distinct kind of satisfaction derived from watching lines of code transform into a functional, usable software system. It's like crafting an elaborate narrative — each function and variable adding a sentence or paragraph to the grand plot. However, writing this novel isn't as simple as putting pen to paper.

Take the example of crafting a 'Hello, World!' application. To the uninitiated, it might seem as simple as this:

```
internal class Program
{
    0 references
    private static void Main(string[] args)
    {
        Console.WriteLine("Hello, World!");
    }
}
```

But those of us in the field know the layers of complexity beneath these simple words: understanding the syntax, setting up the development environment, handling the intricacies of compiling and execution.

4.2   The Pitfalls and Rewards of Coding

Coding is a dance on the razor's edge between creating elegant solutions and descending into a debugging nightmare. Even a minor lapse in concentration can have you chasing after a rogue semicolon like it's the Holy Grail. Consider this block of code:

```
if (isUserLoggedIn = true)
{
    DisplayWelcomeMessage();
}
```

A simple typing error — using a single equals sign (=) instead of a double equals sign (==) — changes an equality check into an assignment operation. The resulting bug can turn an otherwise ordinary day into a debugging marathon.

Yet, despite these pitfalls, the rewards are immense. The thrill of solving a complex problem, the joy of seeing your code run flawlessly

— these are the highs that make the journey worthwhile.

4.3 Funny Coding Blunders and What They Teach Us

Who said coding couldn't be fun? There's a wealth of humor to be found in the blunders we make. Once, a junior developer was asked to "comment their code." The next day, their code was filled with insightful gems like *"// Here, I declared a variable. Cool, right?"*

While we laugh at these anecdotes, they also serve as potent reminders of the importance of clear communication, proper guidance, and precise language in coding.

4.4 Strategies for Efficient and Effective Development

Navigating the intricate process of writing our 'complex novel' certainly poses its challenges, yet it's far from an insurmountable task. By adopting a few effective strategies, we can transform this seemingly daunting endeavor into a manageable, and dare I say, enjoyable one.

Firstly, let's embrace the concept of clean code. Picture this — you're writing your code not just for a machine to interpret, but also for a fellow human being. But this isn't just any person; imagine this individual as a potential violent psychopath who knows where you live, an amusing perspective courtesy of a famous adage by Martin Golding. A far-fetched idea, indeed, but it serves to emphasize the importance of clarity and readability in our code. No matter how cleverly we think we've coded a solution, if it's not easily understood by others *(or by ourselves in a few months)*, then we might be setting up for a meeting with our imaginary psychopath.

However, creating readable code isn't the only aspect we need to consider. We also need to pay close attention to warnings. Those yellow triangles that occasionally pop up in our code editor aren't there for decoration. Even when our code runs without any errors, ignoring these compiler or linter warnings is akin to turning a blind eye to a rickety bridge on a fast-moving train. These warnings serve as our first line of defense against potential issues that may not halt our program but can lead to unintended behavior. They are there for a reason, and heeding their advice is a smart strategy.

Then comes the mantra "test as you go." Waiting until the end to test your code can lead to an agonizing and prolonged debugging process. On the other hand, a test-driven development approach, where we write tests for our code as we develop, can help us identify and squash bugs early in the process. It might seem time-consuming initially, but in the long run, it can save hours, if not days, of debugging headaches.

Finally, remember, version control is your ally, not your adversary. Tools like Git are an invaluable part of a developer's toolkit. These systems allow us to track changes, experiment without fear of breaking our working code, and when things go south, as they invariably do at some point, they are our ticket back to safety. So, make friends with version control, and it will undoubtedly reciprocate in kind when you most need it.

Adopting these strategies can significantly enhance our development process, transforming the task of writing our 'complex novel' from a formidable challenge into an engaging journey of creative problem-solving.

With our complex novel written, it's time to enter the next exciting stage: Testing.

5   Testing: Playing Whack-a-Mole with Bugs

Have you ever played the classic game Whack-a-Mole? It's an apt metaphor for software testing, where, much like the game, bugs pop up unexpectedly from different directions, only to disappear when you try to whack them, and then reappear elsewhere.

If you've ever attempted to release software without proper testing, you'd find yourself in a relentless, not to mention frustrating, game of whack-a-bug. The aim here is not to dampen your spirits, but to underline the significance of this often underestimated phase.

Testing is the unsung hero of software development. It is a vital safeguard that ensures the quality of your software. However, there's a slight caveat - it can quickly transform from a mildly entertaining game of Whack-a-Mole into a nightmare comedy of errors if not performed adequately.

Stories of inadequate testing are plentiful. They may range from the amusing anecdote of a minor bug that made characters in a video game dance uncontrollably, to the less humorous tale of the infamous Mars Climate Orbiter that was lost due to a simple unit conversion error. One cannot help but marvel (and grimace) at the chaos a tiny bug can create.

So, how can we escape this chaos and win the game of Whack-a-Mole?

Firstly, ensure your testing is thorough. *"But we've already tested the major functionalities, isn't that enough?"* you might ask. Not quite. While it's essential to test major functionalities, it's equally important to examine those lesser-used features, edge cases, and error handling.

Automate where you can. Manual testing is tedious, time-consuming, and error-prone. Automation not only expedites the testing process but also reduces the chance of human error. Tools like Selenium and Jest can make your testing life much easier.

Don't forget about regression testing. After you whack a bug, you'd want to ensure that your fix didn't spawn other bugs in the process. Regression testing checks that your recent code changes didn't negatively affect existing functionalities. Lastly, incorporate different types of testing. Unit testing, integration testing, system testing, acceptance testing – they all have their place in the software testing ecosystem. Each of them examines your software from a different angle, providing a well-rounded evaluation of its quality.

Effective testing is not about hunting bugs after the fact; it's about setting up a process where bugs find it hard to hide in the first place. Like a seasoned Whack-a-Mole player, you want to anticipate where the next mole might pop up. It's not an exact science, but with the right strategies in place, you can definitely keep the bugs at bay.

6   Deployment: Watching Your Baby Bird Leave the Nest (or Crash Into a Window)

The moment you've been working towards, the time when your software, your baby bird, is ready to leave the nest and take its first flight. You can't help but swell with anticipation, excitement, and perhaps a hint of *"Torschlusspanik" (a German term for 'gate-closing panic', referring to the fear of missing out or things going wrong at the last minute).*

But let's take a step back. Watching your baby bird leave the nest can go two ways: it might either fly gracefully into the wide, welcoming sky of user acceptance, or it might...well... crash into a window. That's deployment for you - exhilaratingly rewarding when successful, hilariously catastrophic when it goes awry.

Remember the time when an e-commerce giant's website crashed during their much-hyped annual sale? Or *when a popular social media platform experienced a complete blackout on the day of a major global event?* As comical as these incidents may sound in hindsight, they underline the potential disasters that could ensue if deployment isn't handled meticulously.

This brings us to the vital role of contingency plans. You wouldn't send a baby bird off without making sure there's something soft for it to land on in case it fumbles, right? The same goes for your software. Having a solid rollback strategy is just as important as having a deployment plan.

Another key consideration is load testing, especially for applications expected to handle a large user base. This will ensure your software doesn't fold under pressure and leave your users in a lurch *(and you in a state of "Kopfschmerzen" - a German word for a headache).*

And of course, let's not forget the importance of communication during this phase. Keeping your stakeholders informed about the deployment timeline, potential downtimes, and what to expect post-deployment can go a long way in ensuring a smooth transition.

In the end, deploying your software can feel like a high-stakes gamble, an exhilarating mix of nerves and anticipation. But with meticulous planning, thorough testing, and effective communication, you can ensure that your baby bird not only leaves the nest but also soars high in the sky. *Just remember, no matter what happens, there's always a good German word to describe the situation.*

7 Maintenance: The Never-Ending Game of Jenga

Once your software is deployed, you might want to kick back, pour yourself a drink, and breathe a sigh of relief. But alas, the adventure is far from over. Now you're in the realm of maintenance – the unending game of Jenga.

Imagine your software as a meticulously stacked tower of Jenga blocks. Now, each block represents a feature or functionality of your software. Just as with Jenga, every move you make, every block you remove, or add can tip the balance and send your tower tumbling down. That's software maintenance for you, unpredictable, challenging, and yes, a bit like watching a Mr. Bean sketch - filled with comedic chaos that is somehow endearing and nerve-wracking in equal measure.

Imagine Mr. Bean being given the task of maintaining your software. He might understand the basics *(just like he can "drive" his mini)*, but he would probably end up causing a series of hilarious disasters *(much like that time he took an exam, or painted his house, or tried to fix his car)*. While we might laugh at Mr. Bean's antics, in reality, unskilled or careless maintenance can lead to very real, not-so-funny problems.

Take, for example, the seemingly harmless task of updating a piece
of code. In C#, it might look like this:

```csharp
public void UpdateCustomer(Customer customer)
{
    var existingCustomer =
        context.Customers.Find(customer.Id);

    if (existingCustomer == null)
    {
        throw new ArgumentException("Customer does not exist!");
    }

    existingCustomer.Name = customer.Name; existingCustomer.Email = customer.Email;

    context.SaveChanges();
}
```

Now, let's assume that Mr. Bean, in his inimitable style, decides
to ignore the null check. You could end up with an exception:
`NullReferenceException`, which might crash your program and
lead to some significant *Kopfschmerzen* for you and your users.

To avoid such fiascos, it's essential to consider maintenance as a
critical part of the software development life cycle, rather than an
afterthought. Regular updates are crucial for keeping your software
relevant and effective. Proactive troubleshooting can nip problems
in the bud and save you from larger headaches down the line.

Lastly, make sure you document everything! Just like Mr. Bean's
unusual problem-solving methods are documented for our amusement, all software changes should be carefully recorded. This helps
ensure that you, or whoever is maintaining the software in the future,
won't have to spend hours figuring out why a particular change was
made.

So, don't be like Mr. Bean when it comes to maintenance. Be
proactive, be thorough, and remember - this is one game of Jenga

you want to keep going for as long as possible.

8 Summary

In this chapter, we humorously portray the Software Development Life Cycle (SDLC) as a delightful sitcom, offering comedic metaphors for each phase and providing a relatable perspective on the challenges and rewards of software engineering.

2

Coding – It's Just Like Talking to a Toddler

Welcome to the captivating world of coding, a universe where we communicate with machines, making them our allies, our tools, our digital companions. If you think about it, coding is just like having a conversation. However, in this case, it's akin to talking to a toddler. You need to be clear, precise, and quite literally, spell things out. Any ambiguity or complexity could lead to a tantrum, or in coding terms, a system crash or a function failure.

In this chapter, we'll explore this analogy further, unraveling the art of coding communication. From syntax - the grammar of our coding language - to semantics - the meaning and context behind our code. We'll dive into the realm of algorithms, the recipes of our coding world, and finally, delve into the concept of debugging, a form of time travel where we revisit and rectify our past coding mistakes.

1   Syntax: How You Say 'Tomato'

In the wonderful world of coding, syntax holds a paramount role, just like grammar in our spoken language. It provides the fundamental structure of our code. Imagine talking to a toddler using words in a scrambled order. You'd likely get a baffled look, right? That's precisely what happens to a computer when it encounters incorrect syntax - utter confusion.

Different programming languages, much like dialects and accents, pronounce 'tomato' differently. Each one has its unique syntax rules, a framework you need to adhere to if you want your code to make sense. Java's curly braces might feel like home to some, while Python's indentation is a breath of fresh air to others. It's all about learning and adapting to these different ways of saying 'tomato'.

However, just saying 'tomato' correctly isn't enough. You must articulate it in a way that's easy to comprehend. In coding terms, that's ensuring your code readability. Your code should be a clear, comprehensible novel, not a cryptic puzzle. Remember, your future self, and possibly other developers, will thank you for the clarity of thought you bring to your code today.

In our journey of learning syntax, we might encounter hurdles, just like a toddler learning to pronounce 'tomato'. Some common syntax errors might include missing semicolons or unclosed brackets - trivial yet potentially hair-pulling if unnoticed. However, the more you code, the more adept you become at avoiding these potholes. And even when you stumble upon them, you learn to quickly pick yourself up and correct your 'speech'.

2 Semantics: No, The Sky Isn't 'Up', It's 'Above'

Let's continue our toddler-talk adventure into the realm of semantics, which is all about the meaning of what you're trying to express. The semantics of your code are akin to teaching a toddler the difference between 'up' and 'above'. To illustrate, let's take a trip to the beautiful country of Tunisia.

Imagine explaining to a child in Tunisia that the sun is 'up' when you're actually pointing towards a specific spot in the sky. The child, not understanding the difference between 'up' and 'above', might start throwing their toy plane 'up' directly over their head, instead of 'above' towards the sun, causing the toy plane to land somewhere it shouldn't, much to the annoyance of an unsuspecting cat.

Much like this comical miscommunication, improper use of semantics in your code can lead to behaviors that are far from what you intended. Your program might be syntactically perfect, with every bracket and semicolon in its rightful place. *But if your semantics are off?* You're telling your code to throw the toy plane straight 'up', not 'above'. The result? Your program might crash, or worse, produce incorrect results without any warning.

Semantic errors can be insidiously difficult to detect because they don't cause your program to fail in an obvious way. It's like realizing the toy plane was thrown in the wrong direction only after the cat has fled up a tree. That's why it's so important to be mindful of semantics from the outset.

How do you ensure your code's semantics are clear and accurate? For starters, choose meaningful variable and function names that clearly describe their purpose. It's like using the correct words when teaching a toddler. You wouldn't use 'up' and 'above' interchangeably. Similarly, don't name a variable 'counter' if it's actually a placeholder for a customer's name.

Also, aim to write concise functions that carry out a single task. It's easier to understand what a function does *(and spot semantic errors)* when it's not juggling five different tasks. Just like it's easier for a toddler to learn one concept at a time.

Lastly, always understand the context in which your code operates. *Is your code being executed in a loop? Is it handling user input or processing data?* Misunderstanding context can lead to semantic issues. It's like explaining why the sky is 'above' and not 'up' – it makes sense once you understand that 'up' is a direction, while 'above' indicates relative position.

In summary, mastering semantics in coding is as essential as teaching a toddler to use the right words. It may require a bit more effort, but it ensures that your code behaves as expected. *So the next time you code, remember to not just say 'tomato', but to say it right!*

3   Algorithms: The Recipe for Grandma's Soup, Except It Explodes If You Mess It Up

Just as the perfect recipe for grandma's soup can result in a mouthwatering dish, a well-designed algorithm can solve problems efficiently and effectively. An algorithm is like a recipe for your code: it's a step-by-step procedure for performing a task or solving a problem.

The importance and uses of algorithms in coding are widespread. Without them, we wouldn't have Google's search engine, Facebook's news feed, or even the ability to sort a list of numbers in ascending order. It's like having the secret recipe to make grandma's soup - you could try to make it without the recipe, but you're likely to end up with a mess instead of a culinary masterpiece.

For instance, let's consider a simple task of finding the largest number in a list. Here's how you might write the algorithm in C#:

```csharp
public int FindLargestNumber(List<int> numbers)
{
    int largestNumber = numbers[0];

    for (int i = 1; i < numbers.Count; i++)
    {
        if (numbers[i] > largestNumber)
        {
            largestNumber = numbers[i];
        }
    }

    return largestNumber;
}
```

This algorithm goes through each number in the list, checks if it's larger than the current largest number, and if it is, it becomes the new largest number.

Designing effective algorithms requires you to balance between efficiency, simplicity, and flexibility. You want your algorithm to be efficient so it performs the task quickly; you want it to be simple so it's easy to understand and debug; and you want it to be flexible so it can handle a variety of inputs and use cases. But, like messing up grandma's soup recipe by forgetting the salt or overcooking the veggies, things can go horribly wrong if an algorithm isn't correctly implemented.

Take the earlier algorithm for example. *What if the list of numbers is empty?* Our algorithm would throw an exception because it tries to access an element at an index that doesn't exist in the list. This is an example of an algorithmic error. A simple fix would be to check if the list is empty before trying to find the largest number:

```
public int? FindLargestNumber(List<int> numbers)
{
    if (numbers.Count == 0)
    {
        return null;
    }

    int largestNumber = numbers[0];

    for (int i = 1; i < numbers.Count; i++)
    {
        if (numbers[i] > largestNumber)
        {
            largestNumber = numbers[i];
        }
    }

    return largestNumber;
}
```

Just as you wouldn't leave your soup unattended on a high flame, you should always keep an eye out for potential issues when crafting algorithms. Be it a forgotten condition or a misused function, an ill-designed algorithm can lead to major code malfunctions that can be as explosive as grandma's soup recipe going awry.

In conclusion, algorithms are a fundamental aspect of coding. Mastering their design and implementation is a vital part of becoming a skilled programmer. Always remember, a good algorithm is like a well-followed recipe - *it makes sure your code comes out perfectly done every single time!*

4   Debugging: Time Travel to Fix Your Past Mistakes

To many, debugging might feel like an unavoidable, unenjoyable part of coding. To seasoned programmers, it's more akin to time travel. It's a chance to journey back through your past decisions, identify mistakes, learn from them, and set a new course.

The importance of debugging cannot be overstated. It's how we optimize, how we refine, and how we ensure that our code doesn't just run, but runs well. Like learning from past mistakes to better ourselves, debugging refines our code to make it the best version it can be.

There are countless debugging techniques, from setting breakpoints and stepping through your code line-by-line, to writing extensive log files, to simply peppering your code with 'print' statements to track variables' values. The choice of technique often depends on your personal style, the nature of the bug, and sometimes even the mood you're in!

Now, let's talk about a real-world debugging story that, to this day, still brings a smile to the faces of everyone in my Regensburg ex-office.

One of my colleagues, let's call him Klaus, was a stickler for clean, efficient code. One day, he was working on an especially complex algorithm. He was deeply focused, a furrow in his brow, when he compiled his code and ran it. To his surprise, his usually well-behaved code began behaving erratically, like a time bomb with a mind of its own. He checked his algorithm, went through his syntax, and scrutinized his semantics. Nothing seemed amiss.

Klaus decided it was time to debug. He started by setting break-points and tracing through his code. Hours turned into days as Klaus tirelessly dove into the labyrinth of his own creation, searching for the elusive bug.

Meanwhile, the rest of the team watched his relentless pursuit. We all knew the depth of Klaus' determination, but even we were starting to get worried as the fourth day of Klaus' debugging odyssey dawned.

It was on this day, as Klaus sat hunched over his keyboard, that a junior developer walked by, glanced at Klaus' screen, and with a look of innocence only a newbie could have, asked, "Why are you using a semicolon instead of a comma there?" Klaus froze, blinked, and turned slowly to look at his screen. There, in the for-loop that was central to his algorithm, a semicolon was indeed gleefully sitting where a comma should have been. In C#, the semicolon had turned his loop into an empty statement, causing the subsequent code to execute more times than he intended.

In the silence that followed, Klaus let out a roar of laughter that echoed through the office. From that day forward, we often joked about the *semicolon that cost four days.* It served as a great reminder of the importance of a fresh pair of eyes and the need to take breaks when embroiled in intense debugging sessions. So, fellow coders, never forget the art of debugging. Like time travel, it allows us to revisit our past decisions, learn from our mistakes, and avoid potential catastrophes. *And sometimes, it even gives us a great story to tell!*

5 Summary

In this chapter, we've playfully likened coding to the delightful challenge of communicating with a young child. We've underscored the pivotal role of accurate syntax and the clarity of semantics. Just as we take care to ensure our words are comprehensible to a toddler, so too must we ensure our code speaks clearly to a computer. We delved into understanding the essence of algorithms, drawing similarities to the patterns and routines children thrive on. The journey also led us to the often comedic art of debugging, where just as in child-rearing, patience and keen observation are key. Through these whimsical comparisons, we sought to shine a light on the lighter and more amusing facets of software development.

3

The Joy of Version Control

Ever wished life had an undo button, like a misstep at a dance or a misplaced word in a conversation? For us developers, version control is that comforting pat on the back. Dive in with us to discover its magic, from safeguarding our precious code to navigating the tangled web of project branches. Together, we'll tackle the messy bits and celebrate the wins. By the end, you won't just see version control as a tech tool; you'll feel it as a friend in your coding journey. Let's embark on this adventure together!

1 The Basics: If Only You Could Ctrl+Z Your Life

Ever wished you could hit Ctrl+Z after spilling coffee on your favorite shirt or accidentally sending that "reply all" email? In the coding world, version control is our superhero cape, allowing us to undo our missteps and save the day!

1.1   Essentials

Life without version control is like a pizza without cheese – incomplete and just plain wrong. Version control systems are the time machines of the developer world, saving us from past mistakes and ensuring we don't have to relive our coding horrors. They let us "commit" our triumphs and "rollback" our blunders, all with the click of a button. It's like having a guardian angel that watches over our code, ready to swoop in and save the day at a moment's notice.

1.2   Beyond Basics

Once you've gotten the hang of the essentials, it's time to dive deeper into the treasure trove of version control features. It's like unlocking a secret level in a video game where the real fun begins.

Remember that time you felt like a detective in a noir film, sifting through lines of code, looking for that one culprit that broke everything? With version control, you're more like a superhero with time-traveling powers. You can effortlessly travel back in time to when everything was working perfectly, grab the code you need, and bring it back to the present. No more long nights spent cursing at your computer screen!

But that's not all. Version control systems are also like your own personal assistant, keeping track of every change you make. Gone are the days of frantically searching through your code, trying to remember what you did two weeks ago. Now, all you need to do is ask your version control system, and voilà! It's like having a photographic memory at your fingertips.

And let's not forget about branching. This feature allows you to create alternate realities for your code, where you can try out new features or fix bugs without affecting the main project. It's like having your own multiverse, where you can explore different possibilities and choose the one that works best.

So, as you can see, version control is not just a tool for keeping track of changes. It's your partner in crime, your sidekick, and your guide through the tangled web of coding challenges. Embrace it, and watch as your coding life becomes a breeze.

2 Branches: The Multiverse of Your Code

Branching in version control is like opening a portal to a multiverse. Each branch is a different universe where you can experiment, make mistakes, and try out new ideas without messing up the main project. It's like having your own personal playground where the only limit is your imagination.

2.1 Use Cases for Branching

Imagine you're a scientist in a lab, and each branch in your version control system is a different experiment. In this virtual lab, you have unlimited resources and can explore multiple hypotheses at once. Each branch provides a unique environment where you can:

(1) **Test Out New Features:** Just like how a scientist tests a new hypothesis, you can use a branch to develop new features. This is your playground where you can experiment without fear of breaking the main project. It's like having a separate room in

your lab dedicated solely to innovation.

(2) **Fix Bugs:** Every lab has its accidents, and every codebase has its bugs. With branching, you can create a dedicated environment to hunt down and fix those pesky bugs. It's like having a quarantine room where you can isolate the problem, find a cure, and then bring it back to the main project, all without risking contamination.

(3) **Try Out Completely New Ideas:** Sometimes, the most groundbreaking discoveries come from the wildest ideas. Branching gives you the freedom to explore new concepts and approaches, no matter how unconventional they might be. It's like having a secret room in your lab where you can let your imagination run wild and see what happens.

In each of these scenarios, branching provides a safe and controlled environment where you can experiment, learn, and ultimately improve the main project. *And the best part?* If an experiment doesn't work out, you can simply discard the branch and move on to the next one, without any harm done to the main project. It's like having an undo button for your experiments!

2.2 Best Practices for Branching

In the world of branching, just like in a well-run lab, there are certain protocols and etiquettes that ensure everything operates like a well-oiled machine. Here are some best practices to keep your branching experiments successful:

2.2.1 Naming Branches with Purpose

Just as a scientist meticulously labels their test tubes, you need to name your branches in a way that clearly and accurately describes their purpose. Opt for descriptive names that give a clear indication of what the branch is for, such as **"users/mabroukmahdhi/foundations-user-add"** or **"users/andredammeyer/brokers-user-insert"** [1]. This way, you won't find yourself playing detective later on, trying to decipher the mysterious purpose of **"branch1"**.

For those who are interested in diving deeper into the art and science of branch naming, The Standard [2] Community has written a comprehensive guide on best practices for naming branches. This guide is a treasure trove of insights and tips that will take your branching game to the next level. [1] & [2].

Figure 3.1: The engineering Standard for team culture, practices and code of conduct.

---

[1]   Following The-Standard naming convention: users/[username]/[category]-[entity]-[action]

[2]   Hassan Habib's "The Standard" serves as a valuable resource, offering a comprehensive set of guidelines aimed at fostering the development of software systems that are not only maintainable and scalable, but also robust and resilient in the face of evolving challenges.

2.2.2 Merging Back into the Main Project

Once your experiment has concluded, it's time to bring your findings back to the main project. Merge your branches back into the main project in a timely manner, ensuring that your improvements and fixes are incorporated for everyone to benefit from. It's like taking your successful experiment results and applying them to the real world.

2.2.3 Avoiding Sync Issues

Just as a scientist needs to keep their lab equipment calibrated, you need to ensure your branches don't get too far out of sync with the main project. Regularly merge changes from the main project into your branches and vice versa. This helps to avoid conflicts and ensures that your branches are always up-to-date, making the final merge back into the main project a breeze.

By following these guidelines, you'll ensure your branching experiments are always on track and yield the best results. So, put on your lab coat, grab your beaker, and start experimenting with confidence!

3   Merges: Playing Russian Roulette with Your Codebase

Merging in version control is akin to playing a game of Russian Roulette with your codebase. But fear not, dear developer, for with the right strategies and a bit of luck, you'll emerge victorious, unscathed, and with a better, stronger codebase.

3.1　The Basics of Merging

Merging is like creating a beautiful symphony from a cacophony of changes. It brings together all the different notes (changes) from various branches into a harmonious masterpiece. When done right, it can be a thing of beauty; when done wrong, well, let's just say you might need to brace yourself for a cacophony of a different kind.

3.2　Merge Strategies

There are different strategies for this dangerous game. The first is a 'fast-forward merge'. Picture time as a straight line. You start at point A, and while you've moved to point B, Julia hasn't moved. Her changes can be placed directly onto the timeline, fast-forwarding the project to include her work. Simple and elegant, when it works:

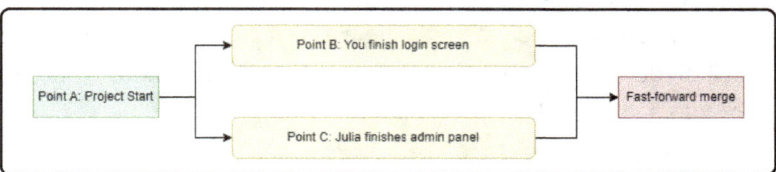

But life, and code, are rarely so straightforward. More often, you and Julia have been working at the same time. The timeline has diverged. In this case, we use a '3-way merge'. The version control system looks at your changes, Julia's changes, and the original code, then tries to blend them together. It's like a cocktail shaker for your codebase.

3.3　Dealing with Merge Conflicts

But what happens when you and Julia have changed the same part of the code? That's a merge conflict, the code equivalent of two people trying to walk through a door at the same time. Resolving these conflicts can be one of the most challenging aspects of using version control. It's a topic so rich *(and potentially traumatizing)* we'll cover it in depth in our next section.

3.4   An Example Merge Process

For now, let's walk through an example merge. You're ready to bring Julia's changes into your branch. In your terminal, you type `git merge julia-branch`. Git begins its magic, merging Julia's changes with yours. If there's a conflict, it'll tell you, giving you a chance to go in, review the disputed code, and decide who wins - your version, Julia's version, or maybe a bit of both.

In essence, merging is the act of reuniting code that has ventured out into different branches for a little while. It can be nerve-wracking, but when done with care, you can bring together disparate pieces of work into a coherent, unified whole.

4   Conflicts: When Your Code Has a Mid-Life Crisis

In version control, conflicts can be seen as the code's mid-life crisis. Imagine two programmers, each armed with their unique coding prowess, working on the same piece of code but having very different ideas about how it should function. When they try to unite their code, the version control system freezes and yells, *"Wait a minute, I'm a tool, not a referee! You guys need to figure this out."* This, dear readers, is the dreaded merge conflict.

4.1 Understanding the Nature of Conflicts

Conflicts in version control are essentially high-stakes games of rock-paper-scissors, where two different changes compete for the same space in the code, and the version control system lacks the wisdom to pick a winner. That's when you, the intrepid coder, step into the limelight.

4.2 Strategies to Avoid Conflicts

Are there strategies to avoid these code duels? Absolutely!

4.2.1 Merging Regularly

One key strategy is to merge regularly. Think of it as a good habit, like eating your veggies. Just as your doctor nags you to eat greens for a healthy body, I'm telling you to merge often to keep your codebase healthy. It allows you to catch potential conflicts early when they're easier to handle.

4.2.2 Effective Communication

Another preventative measure is clear communication within the team. It's vital to know who's working on what so you can coordinate tasks and prevent overlapping work *(and the conflicts that come with it)*. A shared task board or regular team meetings can be a lifesaver here.

4.3 Resolving Conflicts

Despite your best preventive efforts, conflicts may still arise. So, when they do, it's time to play peacekeeper with your code. Most version control systems provide tools and commands that aid in identifying and resolving these conflicts.

In a conflict, the version control system typically highlights the contentious areas in your code. It's then your responsibility to choose which version should prevail or if a blend of both is the solution. Once you've decided, you save the changes and commit them, thereby resolving the conflict.

4.3.1   A Real-world Example

Let's walk through a real-world example: Developers Julia and Nikolai are both working on the same project. Julia has revamped a function to boost performance, while Nikolai has adjusted the same function to squash a bug:

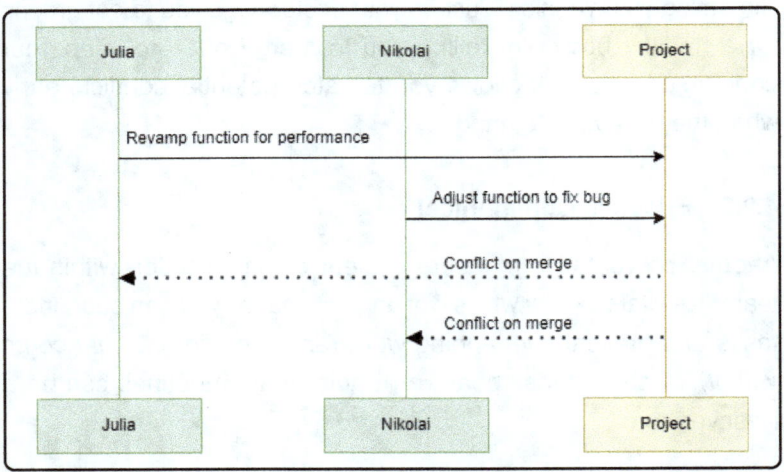

When they try to merge their branches, a conflict arises.

Instead of chaos ensuing, they calmly review the conflicted code together. They conclude that they need a mix of both their changes

– Julia's performance-enhancing refactoring and Nikolai's bug-fixing tweak. They manually merge their code, test the function, and when everything works perfectly, they commit the resolved conflict. Crisis resolved!

4.4   The Silver Lining of Conflicts

Keep in mind that conflict isn't always a bad thing. It necessitates a conversation about what's best for the codebase. So, when your code throws a mid-life crisis, grab your favorite caffeinated beverage and get ready to mediate a peace accord between the clashing lines of code. *And remember, whatever doesn't 'git' you, makes you stronger!*

5   Summary

In this chapter, we explore the pivotal role of version control in software development through a light-hearted lens. Drawing parallels between version control and the fantastical idea of a real-life "Ctrl+Z", we highlight the power it grants developers to rectify errors and journey through diverse code branches. The exhilarating process of merging code and resolving conflicts is humorously likened to playing Russian Roulette with one's code. While maintaining a playful tone, the chapter underscores the crucial nature of version control in overseeing code modifications and fostering teamwork.

4

The Art of Being a 'Software Archaeologist'

Stepping into the world of software development often means inheriting the ancient relics of codebases past. It's a bit like being Indiana Jones, except instead of cracking the code of lost civilizations, we're trying to decipher variables named "xyz123". I know, not quite the hieroglyphics you were hoping for, but trust me, the thrill is real. And unlike poor Dr. Jones, we can't afford to let booby traps (read: bugs) take us by surprise.

This chapter is all about honing your skills as a 'Software Archaeologist', a unique subset of Indiana Jones-like adventurers where the artifacts are chunks of legacy code, the treasure maps are lines of outdated documentation, *and the golden idol?* Well, that's a freshly refactored, well-documented, and efficiently running piece of software.

You know Cleopatra, right? Legendary queen of Egypt, renowned
for her intellect, charm, and the ability to rule an ancient civilization?
Think of legacy code as your own personal Cleopatra. Sure, she
might be speaking an ancient language (COBOL, anyone?), and she
can be somewhat complicated, but with patience, understanding,
and a touch of daring, you can crack the code and rule your software
kingdom with grace.

Just like an archaeologist, you'll need to read, understand, and
preserve the antiquities (legacy code), renovate without destroying
the inherent beauty and function (refactoring), and leave a clear
record for those who come after you (documentation).

In "Cracking the Rosetta Stone," we'll develop an understanding of
legacy code and techniques to make it comprehensible. "Renovating a Haunted Mansion While Living In It" will explore the art of
refactoring without evoking the wrath of hidden specters *(or more
realistically, hidden dependencies).* And in *"Leaving Bread Crumbs
for Your Future (or Someone Else's)"*, we'll ensure your hard work
can be understood by future code explorers through effective documentation.

1   Reading Legacy Code: Unlocking the Enigma Machine

Just like the mysterious and complex Enigma machine used during
WWII [1] for encrypted communication, legacy code can feel like an

---

[1]   World War II.

intricate puzzle waiting to be deciphered. However, with the right approach, you too can crack the code and unravel its mysteries.

1.1   Understanding Legacy Code

So, *what is legacy code?* Think of it as a classic old radio – still functioning but might be challenging to tune in, with frequencies that don't match modern standards. Legacy code, essentially, refers to a codebase or part of it that, despite its age and antiquity, is still operational. However, because of shifts in technology, team dynamics, or programming methods, it can be cumbersome to understand or maintain. Interacting with it can feel like trying to decipher Morse code without a key. But don't fret; we're here to guide you.

Grasping legacy code is akin to eavesdropping on wartime transmissions – the language and protocols might seem foreign, but if you persevere, you'll gain insight into the strategies and decisions of the past. It's a journey into the annals of software history.

1.2   Techniques for Comprehending Legacy Code

Now, onto breaking the code. Just as cryptanalysts in WWII had their techniques, here are some tools of the trade for the modern software 'codebreaker':

- **Debuggers**: Your very own Enigma machine. A debugger lets you step through the code, making sense of each line and function as they execute.
- **System Diagrams**: Think of these as your frequency charts, helping you understand the flow and connections within the system.
- **Code Reading Tools**: These are your decryption tools, giving

you insights into dependencies, metrics, and the overall structure of the legacy code.

1.3   The Importance of Persistence

Just as cryptanalysis demanded persistence, so does understanding legacy code. Embrace the mindset that the code you're diving into was crafted under different contexts and paradigms. See it as a riddle. Every piece you solve leads you closer to comprehending the bigger story.

1.4   Hands-On Examples

Let's now engage with a hands-on example, this time involving C# code. Imagine a function with recursive calls and intertwined if-else conditions, resembling the complex wirings of old communication machines. Fear not; armed with a debugger, determination, and perhaps a system diagram, you'll soon decode its functionality.

Consider the following code snippet:

```csharp
namespace LegacyCodeExample
{
    0 references
    class Program
    {
        0 references
        static void Main(string[] args)
        {
            var result = ComplexFunction(6);
            Console.WriteLine(result);
        }

        5 references
        static string ComplexFunction(object data, int depth = 0)
        {
            if (depth > 10)
                return "Max Recursion Depth Reached";

            if (data is int integerData)
            {
                if (integerData % 2 == 0)
                    return ComplexFunction(integerData / 2, depth + 1);
                else
                    return ComplexFunction(integerData * 3 + 1, depth + 1);
            }
            else if (data is string stringData)
            {
                if (stringData.Length > 5)
                    return ComplexFunction(stringData.Substring(0, 5), depth + 1);
                else
                    return ComplexFunction(stringData.Length, depth + 1);
            }
            else
            {
                return "Unhandled Data Type";
            }
        }
    }
}
```

In this piece, the intertwined if-else conditions and recursive calls might seem convoluted initially. However, by careful tracing and debugging, you can discern the patterns and logic. These conditions and calls might represent different input handling or specific output generation steps.

2   Refactoring: Renovating a Haunted Mansion While Living In It

Just as you'd approach a haunted mansion with caution and a sturdy flashlight, so too must you embark on refactoring legacy code. It might be scary, and it might seem like an insurmountable task, but don't worry, you're not alone. We're here to guide you through it.

2.1   Understanding Refactoring

Before we venture into the mansion, let's first discuss what we mean by "refactoring." Refactoring is the process of altering an existing codebase in a manner that improves its internal structure, readability, or performance, without altering its external behavior. It's like changing the floor plan of a house without changing the façade or the address. In the context of legacy code, it's akin to renovating that haunted mansion without disturbing the spirits (users).

2.2   Identifying Code Smells

In our haunted mansion, *how do we know which rooms need renovating?* In code, we have what we call "code smells," analogous to the mysterious creaks and cold spots in our mansion. Code smells aren't bugs, but they're indications that something might be off. Examples of code smells could include long methods, large classes, duplicate code, or unnecessary complexity. Identifying these gives us a starting point for our refactoring efforts.

2.3   Strategies for Safe Refactoring

Once we've identified the areas that need attention, we need to consider how to refactor safely. After all, we don't want to pull out a supporting beam and have the whole mansion collapse on us:

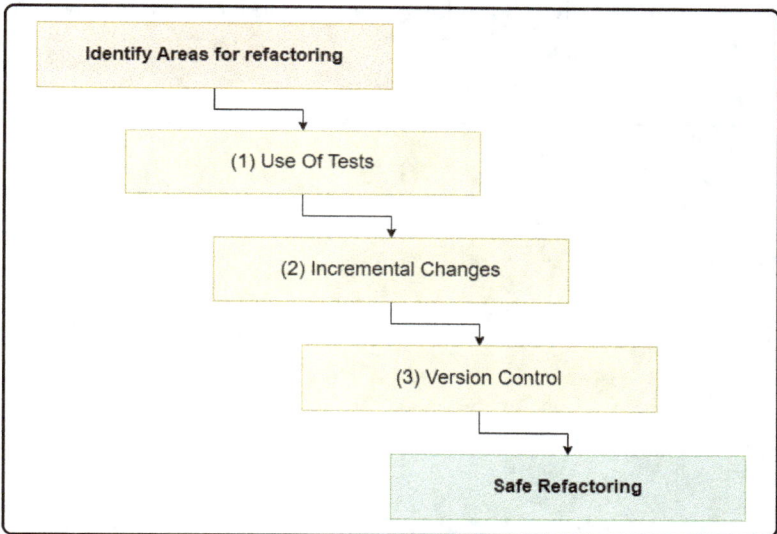

(1) **Use of Tests**: Just as a good ghost hunter never goes in without an EMF meter, you should never refactor without tests. Tests provide a safety net, ensuring that your changes don't accidentally introduce bugs or alter functionality.

(2) **Incremental Changes**: Rather than trying to renovate the entire mansion at once, work on one room at a time. Small, incremental changes are easier to manage and less risky.

(3) **Version Control**: Use version control to track your changes and provide a way to revert if something goes wrong.

2.4   Hands-On Examples

Let's take a practical C# example to illustrate the concept of refactoring with the 'Extract Method' technique. Imagine you have a long and convoluted method that calculates the total cost of items in a shopping cart. It's a classic code smell, like a room in your mansion crammed with antique furniture, making it difficult to navigate. Here's the original code:

```csharp
0 references
static void Main()
{
    // Long method to calculate total cost
    double CalculateTotalCost()
    {
        double subtotal = 0;
        double taxRate = 0.1;
        double shippingFee = 5;

        // Logic to calculate subtotal
        foreach (var item in shoppingCart)
        {
            subtotal += item.Price;
        }

        // Logic to calculate tax amount
        double taxAmount = subtotal * taxRate;

        // Logic to calculate total cost
        double totalCost = subtotal + taxAmount + shippingFee;

        return totalCost;
    }

    double totalCost = CalculateTotalCost();
    Console.WriteLine("Total Cost: $" + totalCost);
}
```

Now, let's apply the 'Extract Method' refactoring to break the method into smaller, more manageable chunks, each with a clear purpose:

```
0 references
static void Main()
{
    double CalculateSubtotal()
    {
        double subtotal = 0;
        foreach (var item in shoppingCart)
        {
            subtotal += item.Price;
        }
        return subtotal;
    }

    double CalculateTaxAmount(double subtotal, double taxRate)
    {
        return subtotal * taxRate;
    }

    double CalculateTotalCost(double subtotal, double taxAmount, double shippingFee)
    {
        return subtotal + taxAmount + shippingFee;
    }

    double taxRate = 0.1;
    double shippingFee = 5;

    double subtotal = CalculateSubtotal();
    double taxAmount = CalculateTaxAmount(subtotal, taxRate);
    double totalCost = CalculateTotalCost(subtotal, taxAmount, shippingFee);

    Console.WriteLine("Total Cost: $" + totalCost);
}
```

By refactoring the code, we've broken the long method into smaller, reusable functions, making the code easier to understand and maintain. Remember, refactoring isn't about getting rid of the old, but about transforming it into something more manageable and elegant. As software archaeologists, we uncover the past and breathe new life into it, ensuring a brighter and less haunted future for our codebase.

3   Documentation: Leaving Bread Crumbs for Your Future (or Someone Else's)

Documentation, the final critical skill in our software archaeology toolkit, is like leaving a trail of bread crumbs for your future self or

other developers who will interact with your code. Good documentation transforms a maze-like haunted mansion into a guided tour,
making navigation much simpler and less daunting.

3.1   The Role of Documentation

Imagine entering an ancient ruin without a map or any clue as to
what the inscriptions on the walls mean. This is how a developer
feels when faced with undocumented legacy code. Good documentation serves as a translator, guide, and blueprint, revealing the
structure and logic behind the code, thus facilitating understanding
and reducing the risk of unintended consequences when modifications are made. It benefits the initial writer by clarifying their thinking,
and it benefits future developers by saving them from hours of code
deciphering.

3.2   Good vs. Bad Documentation

However, not all documentation is created equal. Good documentation is clear, concise, thorough, and regularly updated. It offers
high-level explanations of the system architecture and detailed de-
scriptions of complex logic or algorithms, explaining not just the
'what,' but also the 'why.'

Bad documentation, on the other hand, is vague, incomplete, outdated, or overly verbose. It's like a guide that's speaking in riddles
or an outdated map that leads you to walls where doors used to be.

4   Tools for Documentation

Just as there are many ways to leave bread crumbs, there are
various tools and techniques for documenting your code:

- **Comments in the code**: These are great for explaining tricky sections of code or giving a brief overview of a function's purpose. Remember to keep them updated as code changes!
- **README files**: These provide a high-level overview of the project and typically include information about the system's purpose, how to install and run the code, and any dependencies.
- **Wikis or dedicated documentation software**: These can be used to create more extensive, searchable documentation, including user guides, developer guides, and API documentation.
- **Self-documenting code**: Writing clear, concise, and well-structured code can minimize the need for additional documentation. This can be achieved by using descriptive variable and function names, keeping functions and classes small and focused, and following established coding conventions.

4.1   In Real-Life

We've all encountered projects where excellent documentation made the experience smooth and enjoyable. Conversely, we've faced projects where poor or absent documentation led to confusion, frustration, and significantly more time spent than necessary.

As you journey through the world of software development, remember the value of good documentation. By leaving bread crumbs for your future self and others, you'll not only make your life easier but also contribute positively to the overall health and longevity of the project.

5 Summary

In this chapter, we delve into the fascinating world of 'Software Archaeology,' where we explore the challenges and strategies involved in deciphering legacy code. Much like deciphering the Rosetta Stone, we learn the art of reading legacy code and understanding its historical context. Through "Refactoring," we tackle the daunting task of renovating codebases, akin to living in a haunted mansion while making improvements. Additionally, we emphasize the significance of "Documentation" as a trail of breadcrumbs left for future developers, ensuring smooth transitions and reducing frustration. As software archaeologists, we learn to appreciate the legacy left behind and contribute to the continuous evolution of software systems.

5

Dealing with the Chaos
Monkeys - Software Testing

Navigating the software development world is a bit like charting a course through a dense forest. And in this forest, we often bump into these pesky critters called "Chaos Monkeys." [1] They're not the bad guys; they just test our patience (and our code) every so often. But here's the deal - with the right tools and techniques, we can manage their antics. This chapter will be your field guide, equipping you with everything from the basic shields like unit testing to advanced strategies like continuous testing. And just to keep things engaging, we've woven in some real-world stories of when things went awry.

---

[1] Chaos Monkey is also a tool that was developed by Netflix to test the resilience and reliability of their cloud infrastructure. ***But in this book***, *Chaos Monkey is the unpredictable scenario that threaten to create havoc in a carefully crafted software.*

1   Introduction to Chaos in Software

Picture this: you're crafting a beautiful tapestry *(or, let's say, a pretty epic software)*. Everything's going smoothly, and then – out of nowhere – a monkey jumps onto your workspace, shaking things up! That monkey, my friend, is what we lovingly call a 'Chaos Monkey' in the software realm. And just as its name suggests, it introduces a bit of unpredictability into our otherwise orderly world. *But why do we have such a peculiar name for it, and what's its deal anyway?*

1.1   What are Chaos Monkeys?

Imagine Chaos Monkeys as those cheeky critters in cartoons who love creating a mess. In our tech world, they're like virtual pranksters, intentionally causing little hiccups in our systems. You might be wondering, *"Why on earth would we want that?"* Well, by creating these tiny controlled messes, we can see how our software reacts and fix any weak spots. Think of it as a stress test – but with monkeys! So, even though they might seem a bit pesky, these Chaos Monkeys help us make our software better.

1.2   Why the name 'Chaos Monkeys'?

The fun, jungle-inspired name comes from the idea that monkeys are playful and can be pretty unpredictable. Just like in a jungle where a monkey might suddenly swing by, in our software realm, these Chaos Monkeys pop up and surprise us with unexpected twists. Netflix, the big movie-streaming giant, coined this term because they had a tool that acted just like this – throwing in a little chaos to keep their tech team on their toes. And since then, the name's stuck around, reminding us to always be prepared for those unexpected monkey business moments!

2   The First Line of Defense: Unit Testing

Ever tried to assemble a puzzle and ended up forcing pieces that just don't fit? That's where unit testing steps in for software. It's like taking a moment to inspect each puzzle piece before getting into the bigger picture. Think of unit tests as the safety net, ensuring that when Mr. Bean, in all his endearing chaos, decides to help with your puzzle, you've at least double-checked the corners. And let's face it, in our tech world, a little kuddelmuddel *(that delightful German word for confusion)* is all part of the fun.

2.1   What is Unit Testing?

Unit testing stands as a foundational pillar, essential for ensuring the structural integrity of the final product. At its heart, unit testing is about zeroing in on each individual component, or 'unit', of a software system, and rigorously testing it in isolation. Each unit can be thought of as a singular, distinct part of a larger mechanism.

Let's borrow an analogy from Mr. Bean's iconic adventures with his mini car. Every time he sets out on the road, his car goes through a series of challenges - whether it's navigating through tight spots, avoiding obstacles, or even being driven from an armchair tied to the roof! Now, before Mr. Bean even thinks of such creative endeavors, imagine if he checked each individual part of his car. The brakes, the horn, the wipers, each tire's pressure – ensuring each is working perfectly on its own. Each of these checks symbolizes a unit test, ascertaining that each distinct element functions as it should.

Translating this to software development: before integrating various components or modules together, we methodically test each one in isolation. If a function is devised to calculate a specific result, a unit test would verify this function provides the expected outcome for the given input. It's a process dedicated to validating that each minute part of the software does its designated job flawlessly.

Ensuring the faultless operation of each unit provides a firm foundation for the comprehensive software system. Think of it as making sure each gear in a clock is finely tuned, allowing the whole mechanism to tick away seamlessly. So, unit testing isn't merely about detecting glitches or errors, but constructing software that's dependable, robust, and prepped to handle the curveballs thrown its way. And much like Mr. Bean's meticulous (if unorthodox) car checks lead to entertaining drives, precise unit testing clears the path for impeccable software execution.

2.2   Benefits of Catching the Monkeys Early

There's a certain satisfaction in being one step ahead, *isn't there?* Especially when dealing with those tricky Chaos Monkeys, always waiting in the wings, ready to throw a spanner in the works. These little critters symbolize the unexpected glitches and hitches that can sneak into our software. And if there's one thing we've learned, it's that the sooner we catch them, the better.

Now, let's picture a classic scene from one of Mr. Bean's escapades. *Remember the moments when he's about to make a hilarious blunder?* We, the audience, often spot it coming a mile away, and there's this delightful tension as we wait for the inevitable comedic fallout. But imagine if, just once, someone whispered in his ear before things went haywire, guiding him around the potential mishap. The entire trajectory of his day might change! He'd still be his endearing, bumbling self, but perhaps with a few less calamities under his belt.

That's precisely the advantage of identifying software hiccups early in the process. By spotting and addressing those glitches right at the onset, we set the stage for a more seamless journey ahead. It's akin to preemptively smoothing out the bumps on Mr. Bean's road, ensuring his drive is eventful in all the right ways, rather than a series of mini disasters.

Additionally, there's a certain peace of mind that comes with early detection. It prevents that mad, last-minute dash to fix errors, allowing developers to proceed with confidence, knowing they've already tackled potential pitfalls. And, let's face it, a smooth-sailing project means happier teams, more efficient timelines, and end results that shine.

2.3   When Unit Tests Saved the Day

Each turn reveals new challenges, but also the thrill of unexpected discoveries. And while we relish the victories, it's those near-misses, the "phew" moments, that truly make the journey memorable.

Picture this: A passionate team of developers had poured their heart and soul into creating a state-of-the-art application. Among its myriad of features was a seemingly simple calculator. As the team was dotting the i's and crossing the t's, they stumbled upon a curious anomaly. Instead of multiplying numbers, the calculator was dividing them. Imagine the potential pandemonium if that sneaky bug had slipped into the final product! Visions of befuddled students, frustrated professionals, and a barrage of customer service calls come to mind.

But, in this intricate dance of coding, there's a safety net that often goes unsung – unit tests. This particular bug's spotlight moment was cut short by a meticulously crafted unit test, which flagged the issue before it could make its grand debut. The day was saved, the calculator corrected, and the team breathed a sigh of relief.

This incident serves as a heartwarming testament to the power of thorough testing. In the vast ocean of code, where even a small ripple can create waves, unit tests act as our lighthouses, guiding us safely to our destination. They remind us that, in the world of software, it's not just about building functionalities, but ensuring they stand strong, come what may.

3   Integration Testing: The Big Meetup

Integration testing is the process of combining individual software modules and testing them as a group. Imagine a team of builders working on different rooms of a house. Once each room is complete, they need to ensure that everything fits seamlessly when the rooms are connected. Similarly, in software, after individual units are tested, we need to make sure they function correctly when combined.

3.1   Meeting of Modules: Where Chaos Monkeys Love to Play

Here's where the fun truly begins! Chaos Monkeys absolutely love the spaces between the modules. Why? Because these are places where unexpected behaviors can emerge due to miscommunications, mismatched data, and unpredictable interactions.

For instance, Module A might be expecting data in a particular format which Module B doesn't provide. Or Module C could be triggering a function of Module D too early, causing it to crash. These are the playgrounds where Chaos Monkeys thrive, causing unforeseen problems and merrily dancing on the ruins of our supposedly 'flawless' code.

3.2   The Importance of Integration Tests

To highlight the significance of integration tests, consider the story of a financial app that allowed users to transfer money between their accounts. Unit tests worked perfectly. But, during integration tests, a Chaos Monkey decided to show up. It was discovered that while transferring from savings to checking was flawless, the reverse transaction duplicated the transferred amount. The bug could have been disastrous, resulting in substantial financial discrepancies!

Such incidents underline why it's crucial not only to rely on unit tests but to ensure integrated parts of our software meet up and communicate as expected.

4   Acceptance Tests: The Final Showdown

Acceptance testing is like the final boss battle in a video game. All the minor enemies have been conquered in the earlier stages, but now, you're up against the big one. This is where the code, now polished and integrated, is put to the ultimate test: *Will the stakeholders accept it?* Just as with a video game, before this decisive encounter, you want to stock up on health potions, level up, and perhaps take a few deep breaths.

4.1 Acceptance Tests vs Chaos Monkeys: The Ultimate Battle

Acceptance tests are aimed to ensure that the software system has met the acceptance criteria. Now, Chaos Monkeys, those sneaky creatures, often try their last attempt to wreak havoc in this final stage. They might hide behind user interfaces, lurk in user scenarios, or sometimes masquerade as minor glitches that can create monumental real-world issues. But remember, while Chaos Monkeys are crafty, a well-defined acceptance test is their kryptonite.

4.2 When Acceptance Tests Go Wrong

In all seriousness, while acceptance tests are crucial, sometimes they produce some truly face-palm moments. Like the time an eCommerce site passed all tests but failed to allow users to checkout. Or when a language translation app worked perfectly but translated "Hello, World!" to "Banana, Universe!" in French. Always remember to double-check and perhaps find some humor in the moments of chaos. It makes the journey worthwhile.

5 Performance and Stress Testing

Imagine you've just built a luxurious French château. It's pristine, beautiful, and everything seems perfect. But then, you decide to throw a massive soirée, inviting thousands. Suddenly, the elegant chandeliers are trembling, the hallways are cramped, and the previously enchanting ballroom is suffocating with guests. *Would the château still stand strong or crumble under pressure?* Essentially, that's what performance and stress testing is all about for software.

5.1 Testing under Pressure

Picture this: you're planning the most opulent soirée in that grand French château that you've painstakingly renovated. This isn't just any party; it's the event of the century! Now, as the day draws closer, your heart flutters with both excitement and trepidation. Sure, the invites have been sent, the menu is exquisite, and the château looks picture-perfect. But there's one looming question: *Can it handle the onslaught of excited guests, the hustle and bustle, and the sheer magnitude of the event?*

This scenario is quite similar to unveiling a new software application to the world. You've coded, debugged, and adorned it with features. Yet, much like your opulent soirée, its success depends not just on its elegance and functionality but also on its ability to handle the volume and intensity of its users.

Performance testing, in this context, becomes that essential "dress rehearsal." It's the behind-the-scenes magic that ensures that when the guests arrive in droves, every corner of your château remains impeccable. *Can the ballroom handle the footfalls without a creak? Will the servers, darting between rooms, be able to serve champagne without a single spill?* Similarly, in the digital realm, *can your software handle thousands of users logging in simultaneously?* Will it run smoothly even *when they all decide to hit the 'purchase' button at the same second?*

For software, the stakes are high. Performance testing doesn't just gauge the application's basic functionality. Instead, it meticulously measures how it responds when faced with specific loads or demands. It's not enough for the application to merely "work." It must deliver a seamless experience, ensuring that every feature, every

function, and every facet runs efficiently under the anticipated user
loads.

5.2   Dealing with Heavy Loads

Stress testing, on the other hand, is like seeing how your château
holds up when every single guest decides to jump in sync or start
a conga line across the fragile bridge. It's the "what if" scenario,
pushing software beyond its limits to ensure it doesn't just collapse
in a heap when things get a little out of hand. If performance testing
is about grace under pressure, stress testing is about survival during
a full-on "baguette" duel.

Stress testing is vital because, in the world of software, there are
always those unpredictable moments when user loads skyrocket
or when unprecedented scenarios occur. The last thing you'd want
is for your software to throw in the white flag just when things get
interesting.

Your software might be functioning perfectly under normal conditions,
but in the grand soirees of the digital world, you never know when a
random 'baguette' duel might break out. Better be prepared than
sorry!

6   Maximizing Efficiency: Tips for Cost-Effective Testing

As we navigate through the forest of software testing, let's not forget
our wallets. Testing, while essential, doesn't have to break the bank.
Here are some pro tips to keep your testing endeavors both efficient
and economical. Testing is much like shopping for a new wardrobe.

You want the best bang for your buck, ensuring you're not splurging on unnecessary items while still looking fabulous.

6.1 Prioritize Testing Efforts

Imagine your software as a big, strong castle. It's your job to keep it safe from the Chaos Monkeys, who are like cheeky invaders trying to sneak in. *You wouldn't leave the front door open while you're busy cleaning the spoons in the dining room, right?*

The main goal is to figure out which parts of your software need the most testing to keep it safe from Chaos Monkeys. Start by figuring out which parts are most likely to have problems and which ones would be the biggest deal if they didn't work right.

Once you know what the most important parts are, you need to focus on testing them really well to make sure they can handle anything the Chaos Monkeys throw at them.

But don't forget about the other parts of your software, too! They need some testing as well, just like you wouldn't leave the back door of your castle open for invaders. Even if they're not the most important parts, they still play a role in keeping your software safe.

By being smart about where you put your testing efforts, you can make sure your software is strong, safe, and ready for anything.

6.2 Reuse Test Cases

Ever donned the same classic black dress or sleek suit to multiple soirées, simply jazzing it up with different accessories each time? Just as our wardrobe can be versatile, so can our test cases. The practice of reusing test cases is akin to repurposing that timeless outfit – it's practical, efficient, and just plain smart.

When we craft a test case, we're investing time and effort into ensuring it thoroughly examines a specific functionality or aspect of our software. It's a meticulously tailored suit, perfectly fitted to our needs. But just as a well-made suit can be worn to various events, a well-crafted test case can be reused for different versions or iterations of our software.

The beauty of reusing test cases lies in its simplicity. Once a test case is created, it can be stored in a repository, ready to be pulled out and dusted off whenever needed. When a new version of the software is developed, these test cases can be easily adapted and reused, saving us the time and effort of creating new test cases from scratch.

But wait, there's more! Reusing test cases also ensures consistency in testing. Just as wearing the same outfit to different parties provides a consistent image, reusing test cases ensures that the same functionalities are tested in the same way, regardless of the software version. This consistency is crucial in maintaining the quality and reliability of the software over time.

And let's not forget about the ease of maintenance. When test cases are reused, any updates or changes can be made in one place, and these changes will automatically be applied to all versions of the software being tested. It's like updating your wardrobe with a new accessory, and voilà, your outfit is refreshed and ready to make a statement.

In conclusion, reusing test cases is like having a wardrobe filled with versatile and timeless pieces. It's a smart and efficient way to ensure that your software is always dressed to impress, ready to take on any Chaos Monkeys that dare to crash the party. So go ahead, start building your repertoire of test cases, and watch as they become the MVPs of your testing toolkit.

6.3 Optimize Test Environments

Managing test environments is akin to hosting a lavish dinner party. Just as you wouldn't dream of serving your guests a gourmet meal on paper plates with plastic forks, you must ensure that your test environments are carefully curated and optimized to provide accurate and reliable results.

Think of your test environment as the grand dining hall of a royal castle. This hall must be meticulously prepared to accommodate the diverse needs of your noble guests (test cases). It should be equipped with the finest silverware (tools) and adorned with the most exquisite tapestries (data) to ensure a sumptuous feast (successful testing).

Here are some tips to optimize your test environments:

(1) **Standardize Your Environments**: Just as you would have a consistent theme for your dinner party, standardize your test environments to ensure consistency across different testing phases. This includes using the same operating systems, software versions, and configurations.

(2) **Use Realistic Data**: The same way a chef uses the finest ingredients to prepare a meal, use realistic and relevant data in your test environments. This ensures that the testing is reflective of real-world scenarios and provides valuable insights.

(3) **Keep Environments Isolated**: Just as you wouldn't want the dessert to mix with the appetizers, keep your test environments

isolated from each other to prevent any interference and ensure accurate results.

(4) **Maintain a Clean Environment**: Just as a clean and tidy dining hall enhances the dining experience, maintain a clean and organized test environment. Regularly update and patch software, remove unnecessary data, and ensure that all tools are functioning correctly.

(5) **Monitor and Analyze Results**: Just as you would seek feedback from your guests after a dinner party, monitor and analyze the results of your testing. Use tools and metrics to assess the performance of your test environments and make necessary improvements.

By optimizing your test environments, you can ensure that they provide a fertile ground for your test cases to flourish, ultimately leading to more accurate and reliable testing results. So, go ahead, roll out the red carpet, and let your test environments shine as the stars of the show, ready to tackle any Chaos Monkeys that dare to disrupt the performance.

6.4   Continuously Monitor and Improve Testing Processes

Testing is indeed an ongoing feast, not just a one-time lavish banquet. To truly savor the flavors of success, we must regularly review and refine our testing processes, using a variety of metrics and tools to assess their effectiveness, much like a master chef who tweaks and perfects recipes until they're just right.

Imagine your testing process as a series of intricate dishes being prepared for a grand culinary competition. Each dish (test) must be meticulously crafted and evaluated to ensure it meets the highest standards of quality and excellence. But the work doesn't stop there. Just as a chef tastes and adjusts the seasoning of a dish, we must continuously monitor and fine-tune our testing processes to achieve the desired results.

Here are some ways to continuously monitor and improve your testing processes:

(1) **Use Metrics and KPIs**: Just as a chef relies on precise measurements to create a perfect dish, use metrics and key performance indicators (KPIs) to quantitatively assess the effectiveness of your testing processes. These could include metrics such as test pass rate, defect density, and testing efficiency.

(2) **Gather Feedback**: Just as a chef values feedback from diners, gather feedback from stakeholders, developers, and testers to gain insights into the strengths and weaknesses of your testing processes. Use this feedback to make necessary improvements.

(3) **Conduct Regular Audits**: Just as a restaurant undergoes regular health inspections, conduct regular audits of your testing processes to ensure they are compliant with industry standards and best practices.

(4) **Embrace Automation**: Just as a chef uses modern kitchen appliances to enhance efficiency, embrace automation to streamline your testing processes. Use automated testing tools to reduce manual effort and increase accuracy.

(5) **Stay Updated with Latest Trends**: Just as a chef stays abreast of the latest culinary trends, stay updated with the latest trends and advancements in software testing. Attend conferences, participate in webinars, and read industry publications to continuously improve your testing processes.

By continuously monitoring and improving your testing processes, you ensure that they remain effective and efficient, much like a chef who perfects a recipe over time. This ongoing commitment to excellence will ultimately lead to a software application that is robust, reliable, and ready to face the world, free from the mischief of any Chaos Monkeys that dare to test its mettle.

7 Summary

Our journey through the realm of software testing has given us a profound appreciation for those elusive Chaos Monkeys. These critters, always poised to cause mayhem, have underscored the importance of thorough testing at every stage. We've seen how Unit Testing is our early-warning system, catching problems before they escalate. Integration Testing then ensures that as our code modules convene, they do so harmoniously, without any monkey business. Acceptance Tests are our litmus test for software readiness, and Performance and Stress Testing confirm our software's resilience, even under monkey-induced pandemonium.

6

The Wonderful World of Deployment

In this chapter, we'll set sail on a mesmerizing journey through the magical worlds of **Continuous Integration** and **Continuous Deployment**. In these places, automation is like the spellbinding sorcerer, making even the most daunting tasks feel like a graceful waltz.

Then, imagine us heading to the warm embrace of Containers – think of them as luxury suites for your code. Here, every bit of software is pampered like a star, nestled in its very own special setting.

And as we wrap up our delightful evening, let's channel our inner overprotective yet loving parent vibes in the realm of Monitoring. Together, we'll master the gentle craft of watching over our precious code kiddos, making sure they play nice when we send them out to explore the vast digital playground.

1   CI/CD: Automating the Scary Stuff

The scary stuff - when our beautiful, painstakingly written code has to leave the cozy, predictable confines of our local machines and face the wild, wild west of production. That's where Continuous Integration and Continuous Deployment (CI/CD), our unsung heroes, swoop in to save the day. Think of CI/CD as the trusted bodyguard escorting our code safely from development to deployment, ensuring it doesn't stumble and trip over in the process.

CI/CD are like the peanut butter and jelly of software deployment - an inseparable duo that transform the often-dreaded deployment process into a streamlined, pain-free experience. They're the magical behind-the-scenes elves that work tirelessly, catching issues, testing, building, and deploying. With CI/CD, there's no more fretting over a feature that worked perfectly on your local machine but decided to throw tantrums in the live environment. It's like having a trusty assembly line that ensures every code piece that leaves your local machine is always in its best form, ready to put on a show in production.

1.1   Unveiling the CI Process

Step into the mesmerizing realm of Continuous Integration (CI), where your code is under the vigilant gaze of an inspector who leaves no stone unturned. It's like a skilled detective meticulously examining every clue before a case can proceed. As we delve into this subsection, prepare to unravel the intricate mechanisms that orchestrate the CI process.

Picture a virtual assembly line where each piece of code is meticulously tested, refined, and polished before it's allowed to continue its journey. Automated tests are the unsung heroes here, subjecting your code to a battery of trials to ensure its functionality is flawless. Think of them as the meticulous taste-testers in a gourmet kitchen, ensuring that every dish leaving the kitchen is perfect.

But it's not just about functionality; it's also about maintaining the highest quality standards. Linters, akin to meticulous editors, review your code's grammar, style, and organization. They ensure your codebase speaks a consistent and coherent language, just like a symphony's harmonious notes.

1.2   The Dance of Continuous Deployment

Continuous Deployment (CD) is an elegant ballet of processes, technologies, and best practices that allows software changes to be automatically deployed to a production environment after passing through various stages of testing. Like a dance that demands perfect synchronization among the dancers, CD requires seamless integration among development, operations, and quality assurance teams. Let's delve into this intricate dance, step by step.

1.2.1   The Choreography: Understanding the Process

Every dance has a choreography, a series of steps that must be executed in a particular order to create a harmonious performance. In the world of CD:

• **Code Commit**: Developers write and commit the code to the version control system.

- **Automated Build**: On every commit, automated tools build the software, ensuring it's free from basic compilation errors.
- **Unit Tests**: These are quick, isolated tests that verify individual units of code.
- **Integration Tests**: Check how newly committed code interacts with existing components.
- **Acceptance Tests**: These tests assess if the software behaves as intended from a user's perspective.
- **Deployment**: If the software passes all tests, it is automatically deployed to the production environment.

1.2.2 The Music: Tools & Technologies

Like a dancer needs music to set the pace and mood, CD leans heavily on tools and platforms. Some leading players in the space are Jenkins, Travis CI, CircleCI, and GitHub Actions. Docker and Kubernetes can also play pivotal roles in ensuring consistency in deployments across various environments.

1.2.3 Graceful Recovery: Handling Failures

Even the best dancers occasionally miss a step. The key is how they recover. Similarly, not every deployment will be perfect. Automated rollback mechanisms can help in restoring the last stable version if something goes awry. Monitoring *(More details in the section 3)* and logging tools like Grafana, ELK Stack, and Prometheus can aid in quick detection of anomalies post-deployment.

1.2.4 The Dancers: Roles & Responsibilities

In CD, the roles are not limited to just developers or operations teams. Everyone is a dancer, and each one plays a vital role:

- **Developers**: Write clean, testable code and commit frequently.
- **QA Engineers**: Ensure that tests cover all possible scenarios and are updated as the software evolves.
- **Operations**: Maintain the infrastructure, ensuring that deployment tools and environments are always in an optimal state.
- **Security Teams**: Continuously monitor and safeguard the process against potential vulnerabilities.

1.2.5   Rehearsal: The Importance of Staging

No dance performance is staged without rehearsals. Likewise, before deploying to production, it's wise to deploy to a staging environment that closely mimics production. This provides a final sanity check and offers a safety net against unforeseen issues.

1.2.6   The Finale: Continuous Feedback Loop

The dance of Continuous Deployment doesn't end with the software going live. The feedback from monitoring tools, end-users, and internal teams is invaluable. This feedback is what drives the next iteration, making the dance of CD a never-ending loop of improvement.

In conclusion, like every masterful dance, Continuous Deployment is a harmonious blend of precision, coordination, and agility. It transforms the mundane process of software delivery into an orchestrated performance, ensuring that users always experience the best version of the product.

2   Containers: Your Code's Personal Hotel Room

Imagine this: After a tiring journey, you check into a luxurious hotel room. It's isolated, self-contained, and has everything you need for a comfortable stay. This is exactly what containers offer to your code – a cozy, well-equipped environment that runs consistently across various stages of deployment. Let's unpack this "hotel experience" for your software.

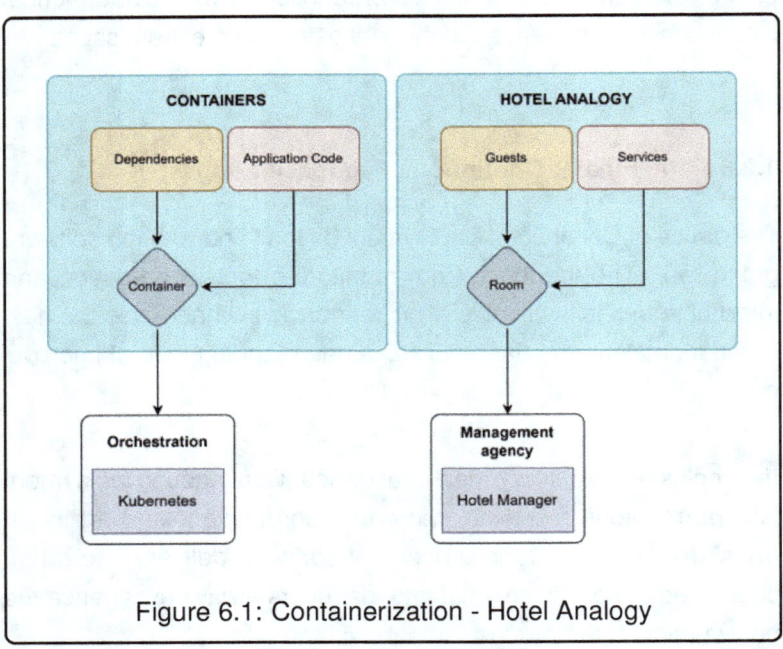

Figure 6.1: Containerization - Hotel Analogy

2.1   Check-In: Image Creation

The process of preparing an application for deployment can be likened to getting ready for a hotel stay. Just as you might make a reservation for a specific type of room with particular amenities, in the world of containerized deployments, we begin with something called an image specification.

This image specification, often compared to a "reservation slip" or checklist, is your way of stating exactly what your application needs to run properly. In the realm of Docker [1], this checklist is known as a Dockerfile. It outlines everything from the software your app requires to certain settings it might need to function at its best.

After drafting this checklist, the next step is to create or "build" this image. Imagine it as setting up and packing a suitcase with everything you'd need for your hotel stay. Once this image is crafted, it can be taken or "checked-in" to different environments, much like how you can check into different hotels with your suitcase. The beauty of this process is that by having a consistent "suitcase", or in this case, image, you're ensuring that your application has everything it needs, no matter where it's deployed.

To make this concept even more relatable, think of popular online platforms where you might reserve a hotel room. Before booking, you specify whether you want a single or double bed, if you need Wi-Fi, or perhaps a room with a view. Similarly, your image specification outlines all the conditions for your application to operate effectively.

---

[1]   Docker: A popular tool for containerization

2.2   Room Service: Dependency Management

Think of the many times you've stayed in a hotel and browsed through the room service menu. Maybe it's a craving for a slice of cheesecake at midnight or a strong cup of coffee early in the morning. No matter the request or the time, the hotel, with its room service, is ready to cater to your specific needs. In the world of software, this "always-ready-to-serve" concept mirrors how containers manage dependencies for your application.

Dependencies can be thought of as those special requests or necessities your application needs to function optimally. Just like how you might have a penchant for a specific brand of tea or a particular type of pillow, your application too may have preferences in terms of software libraries, versions, or configurations.

Containers act like the ever-reliable hotel room service, ensuring that these dependencies are always available to your application. They guarantee that everything runs smoothly, irrespective of where or when the application is deployed. So, if an application is like a guest in a hotel, the container ensures it always has its preferred amenities on hand.

Furthermore, this approach eliminates the notorious "*It worked on my machine!*" scenarios, where developers find discrepancies in application behavior across different environments. Going back to our hotel analogy, it would be like a guest being upset because they couldn't find their hometown's local snack in the minibar. By setting a standard "menu" or environment through containers, developers ensure that the application's experience is consistent, no matter where it checks in.

2.3 Housekeeping: Isolation & Security

Imagine the sense of privacy and security you feel when you step into your hotel room and lock the door behind you. Within that room, you have your own space, devoid of any interference from fellow guests. The bed is yours, the bathroom is yours, and the entire ambiance is tailored for your comfort. This encapsulated experience of having a personal space in a hotel mirrors the principle behind the containers in the software realm.

Containers are designed to grant each application its own private "room" or environment. In this dedicated space, the application has all it requires to function without being disturbed by other "guests" or applications. This isolation ensures there are no clashes or conflicts with other software, akin to the peace you experience without noisy neighbors in a hotel.

Moreover, just as hotel rooms have locks, safes, and sometimes even security systems to protect your belongings and ensure your safety, containers offer security boundaries for applications. Each container functions independently; therefore, should any security issue arise within one container, the problem remains confined to that "room" without affecting its neighbors. Think of it as a spill in one hotel room that doesn't seep into the adjacent rooms, ensuring each guest's environment remains unaffected.

To extend the analogy, imagine if, in a hotel, one room had a plumbing issue. This issue would not cause the taps in other rooms to stop working. Similarly, if one container faces a malfunction or security breach, it won't disrupt the functioning of other containers.

2.4   Checkout & Room Transfers: Portability

Picture this: you've had a pleasant stay in a luxury suite in Paris, and a week later, you find yourself in a suite of the same hotel chain in Sydney. To your delight, the layout, the amenities, and the overall experience are strikingly familiar, even though you're thousands of miles away. This sense of consistent comfort and familiarity, regardless of location, is much like the promise of container technology in software deployment.

Containers encapsulate the essence of portability. Just as a hotel chain ensures a standard experience across its branches worldwide, a container preserves the environment and settings of an application. This means an application can seamlessly "check out" from a developer's local setup and "check in" to diverse environments, such as testing servers, staging areas, or even production sites. The transition is smooth, and the application feels "at home" irrespective of where it's deployed.

Such portability eradicates the commonly dreaded phrase in software development: "It works on my machine." The reason? With containers, the application essentially carries its "room" or environment with it. Every necessary configuration, every specific setting, and every dependency travels with the application. It's akin to having a hotel room that can be lifted and placed anywhere in the world, yet the inside of the room remains unchanged.

In a broader perspective, just as hotel chains aim to offer a unified experience to guests across the globe, containers strive to provide a consistent runtime environment for applications. This ensures that developers and users alike can anticipate predictable behavior, no matter where the application is "checked in."

2.5 Overbooking: Orchestration

Imagine arriving at a luxury hotel after a tiring journey, only to find out it's overbooked. Panic ensues. Now, picture a scenario where the hotel manager snaps their fingers, and instantly a new room appears, tailored exactly to your booking specifications. No fuss, no stress, just seamless accommodation. While this might sound like a dream in the world of hospitality, in the realm of software containers, it's very much a reality.

Orchestration tools, with Kubernetes being a prime example, act as these magical hotel managers. They monitor the demands on applications and ensure that containers – akin to hotel rooms – are provided or removed based on the needs. If there's a surge in users or requests *(much like a hotel facing a sudden influx of guests)*, the orchestrator scales up the number of containers to ensure every "guest" or request is accommodated. Conversely, during quieter periods or off-peak hours, it scales down, optimizing resources.

The brilliance of orchestrators lies in their ability to maintain a balance. They ensure applications are equipped to handle high demand without crashing *(no turning away of guests)* while also being resource-efficient during lulls *(not wasting electricity on lighting up empty rooms)*. It's a dynamic and responsive system that adjusts in real-time.

Moreover, just as a seasoned hotel manager might move guests to more appropriate rooms based on specific needs or preferences, orchestrators can distribute and manage containers across various machines or clusters, ensuring optimal performance and resilience.

2.6   Loyalty Programs: Ecosystem & Community

Frequent travelers often stick to certain hotel chains because of the perks and a sense of familiarity. Similarly, the container ecosystem, with tools like Docker and Kubernetes, has built a loyal community of developers. Regular updates, a vast library of pre-built images, and community support make it the "go-to hotel chain" for many software applications.

In conclusion, containers offer your code the luxury and predictability of a five-star hotel experience. They ensure that your application runs in a comfortable, consistent environment, no matter where it's deployed. So, the next time someone asks about containers, just say, "It's like giving your code a VIP hotel treatment!" And who wouldn't want that? Safe travels in the container world!

3   Monitoring: Keeping a Paranoid Eye on Your Code Children

Deploying an application is much like sending your beloved child to their first day at school. You've nurtured it, you've seen it grow, and now it's time to let it face the real world. But, what's a parent without a bit of paranoia? In the world of deployment, this paranoia manifests as monitoring. And oh boy, are we serious about it!

3.1   Why Monitor?

Imagine the time and energy you've devoted to your software as the countless hours you'd pour into raising a little one. From its birth (initial commits) to its turbulent teenage years (debugging sessions), you've been there every step of the way. Monitoring is the equivalent of keeping a vigilant eye out for your child while ensuring they're navigating the world correctly. *Let's delve deeper into this world, shall we?*

3.1.1 The Heartbeat of Your Application

Much like listening to the gentle heartbeat of a sleeping child, monitoring gives you a constant pulse on your software's health. Think about how a sudden silence or an accelerated rhythm can induce panic for a parent; similarly, unexpected silence from a server or rapid spikes in user traffic can be equally nerve-wracking for a developer.

Example: Consider an e-commerce platform on Black Friday. Without proper monitoring, the sudden influx of users *(akin to a toddler's sugar rush)* can bring down the entire platform. With monitoring, you can watch for those increases in traffic and scale accordingly, preventing meltdowns.

3.1.2 Crash Analysis

Children are notorious for throwing tantrums for seemingly no reason, just like applications that crash without an obvious trigger. Monitoring offers insights into what's provoking these outbursts. *Was it a new feature you added? Or perhaps an unhandled exception?*

Example: Spotify once faced an issue where their application consumed excessive disk space. It turned out that a minor bug was writing massive amounts of junk data. Continuous monitoring was what caught this anomaly in data usage patterns, allowing them to promptly rectify it.

3.1.3   Scaling and Load Issues

When your kid's popular in school, you need a bigger carpool. Similarly, when your application gets more user love (traffic), you need better resources. We can visualize it like this:

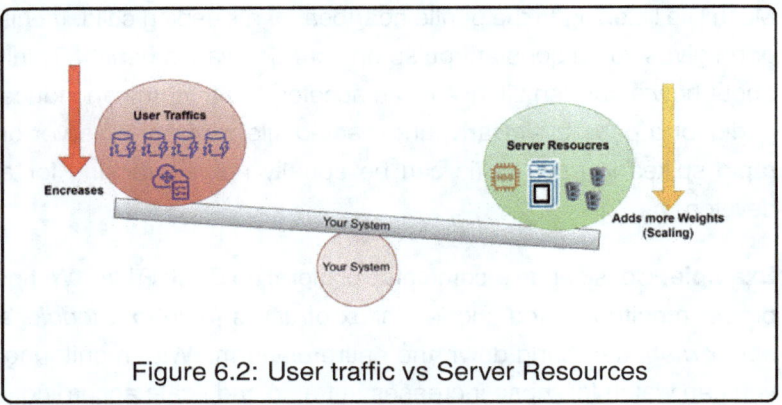

Figure 6.2: User traffic vs Server Resources

Monitoring helps you see these popularity trends and prepare for them.

The Overachievers and the Procrastinators: Performance Metrics Every parent knows their kid's strengths and weaknesses. Similarly, through monitoring, you know which parts of your application excel and which ones lag.

Example: Netflix uses real-time monitoring to ensure smooth streaming for its users. When they notice specific content pieces or regions experiencing lag, they can redistribute resources to enhance viewer experience.

3.1.4   Historical Data and Analysis

Remembering your child's first steps or their first word is precious. Likewise, in the tech realm, historical data provides invaluable insights into how your application behaved over time, helping in future optimizations.

Check the following timeline example:

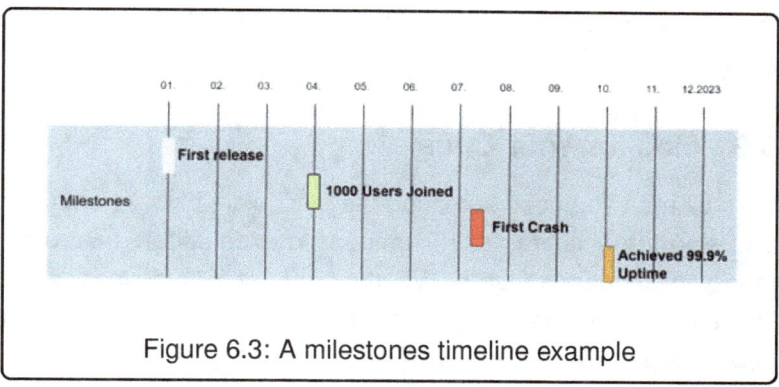

Figure 6.3: A milestones timeline example

This timeline (Figure 6.3) is punctuated by significant events, or 'milestones', that represent both achievements and challenges in the application's lifecycle.

(1) **First Release:** This marks the birth or the debut of the application, the point where it was first introduced to the world.
(2) **1000 Users Joined:** An early sign of user adoption and interest, indicating the application is gaining traction and resonating with its intended audience.
(3) **First Crash:** A challenging setback. This milestone signifies the application's first major hiccup, emphasizing the inevitable obstacles any software will face.
(4) **Achieved 99.9% Uptime:** A celebratory achievement, show-

casing the application's stability and reliability over time. This suggests that, post the initial hiccups *(like the aforementioned crash)*, measures have been taken to ensure consistent availability.

In conclusion, monitoring isn't just a technical necessity—it's an emotional one. It provides peace of mind, allowing you to react proactively rather than being always on the defensive. After all, being there for your application's highs and lows is what tech parenting is all about!

3.2   Monitor Your Code

Let's be real: you need some top-tier binoculars if you're planning on being the ultimate nosy neighbor. In code-speak, this refers to top-tier monitoring tools. Whether you opt for old classics like Nagios and Graphite, or you're more of a New Relic and Datadog person, ensure that your tool:

- Gives real-time data *(because waiting is for chumps)*.
- Offers historical insights *(to reminisce about those CPU spikes on Christmas Eve)*.
- Can send alerts *(basically, the digital equivalent of your neighbor ringing the bell to notify you of misbehaving kids)*.

3.3   Metrics

In the vast universe of software, metrics are the equivalent of the gold stars you'd receive on your homework. But these aren't just fancy stickers; they're vital indicators of your application's health and performance. Let's put on our proud parent hats and dive deeper into these digital report cards.

3.3.1   CPU Usage

Imagine a teenager guzzling energy drinks one after the other. That's your application with high CPU usage.

Details: CPU usage indicates the percentage of processing power being used by your application. A consistently high CPU usage can indicate that your code may not be optimized or there's a rogue process.

Example: Let's say a video game suddenly starts consuming 90% of the CPU. The gameplay would become choppy, and other applications might freeze. Continuous monitoring might reveal that a particular graphic render or an unoptimized loop is the culprit.

Now, check this:

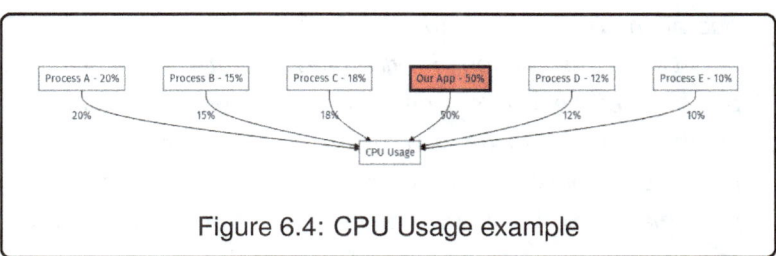

Figure 6.4: CPU Usage example

From the graph, it's evident that the process labeled 'Our App' consumes a significantly higher percentage of CPU resources, clocking in at 50%. This is in stark contrast to other processes like 'Process A', 'Process B', and so on, which have a much lower CPU usage ranging from 10% to 20%.

Such a disproportionate consumption of CPU resources by a single process can lead to several issues:

(1) **Performance Bottlenecks:** The application may become the

primary source of system slowdowns, leading to reduced overall system performance.

(2) **Reduced Multi-tasking Efficiency:** Other processes might be starved of necessary CPU cycles, causing them to run slower or even freeze.

(3) **Increased Power Consumption:** On mobile or battery-operated devices, higher CPU usage can lead to faster battery drain.

The visual emphasis on 'Our App' with a distinct color and width serves as a visual cue, highlighting the urgency of optimization. The exclamation mark or other visual representations, such as 'screaming,' further accentuates the critical nature of this issue.

> **Recommendation:** *In such real cases, developers and system architects should delve deeper into the functionalities and operations of 'Our App' to identify the root causes of such high CPU consumption. Profiling tools can be employed to pinpoint inefficient code segments or operations that might be contributing to this excessive usage. Once identified, optimization strategies, such as code refactoring, algorithmic improvements, or even hardware upgrades, can be considered to bring the CPU consumption of 'Our App' in line with other processes.*

3.3.2   Memory Consumption

Memory consumption is all about how much data your application needs to store in RAM for it to function efficiently. Just as our brains can only handle so many tasks at once, an application has a limit to how much it can remember at a given time. Crossing this limit could lead to performance issues or even crashes.

Example: Think of a browser with 50 tabs open. Each tab consumes a bit of memory. If the combined consumption exceeds the available RAM, the system starts to slow down, causing lags or freezes.

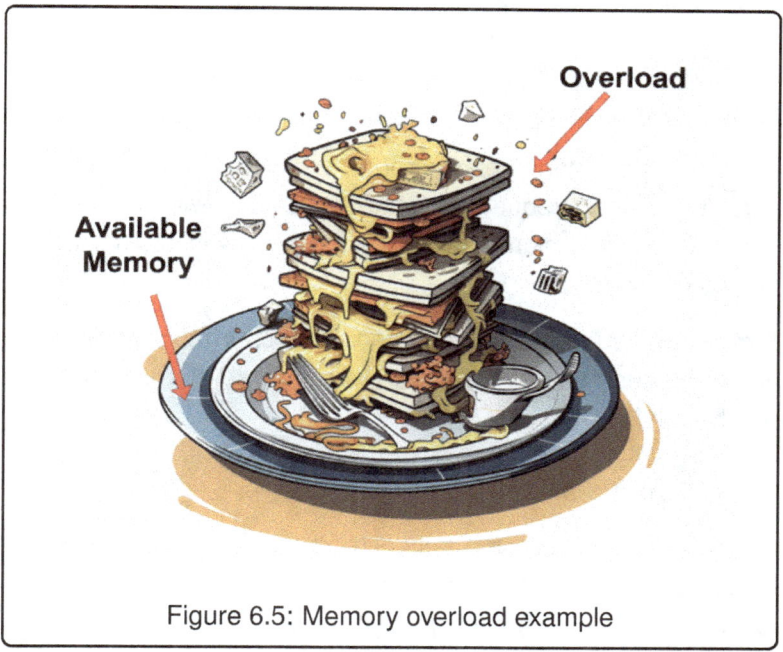

Figure 6.5: Memory overload example

In this visual representation (Figure 6.5) of the food spilling over from the plate symbolizes the overload, indicating that the system is nearing or has exceeded its memory capacity.

- **Memory Overload:** When the used RAM approaches or exceeds the total available RAM, it signifies a memory overload. This can lead to performance issues, as the system may resort to using slower secondary storage (like hard drives) as a makeshift RAM, a process known as paging or swapping.

- **Optimization:** Regular monitoring of memory usage can help in identifying memory-hungry applications or processes. Once identified, these can be optimized or closed to free up RAM.
- **Upgrades:** In systems that consistently experience memory overloads, it might be beneficial to consider upgrading the RAM to accommodate the growing needs.

3.3.3   Response Times

Response time measures the speed at which your application responds to a user's requests. It's the difference between a webpage that loads almost instantly and one that leaves users drumming their fingers on the table.

Example: Two online stores. Store A loads in 2 seconds, while Store B takes 10 seconds. Users are likely to abandon Store B, resulting in lost sales.

3.3.4   Error Rates

Just as detention notices at school alert parents to potential misbehavior, error rates in the digital realm serve as cautionary signals for developers. While occasional hiccups are par for the course, consistently high error rates wave a bright red flag. For instance, consider an online bank application: if it frequently stumbles during money transfers, it's not only going to exasperate its users but also tarnish the trust they place in the platform, leading to potential damage to the brand's reputation.

These metrics, like silent alarms, convey your application's performance tales. They might reveal moments of sheer brilliance or desperate cries for help. The key lies in attuning oneself to these narratives, ensuring that your software not only excels but also evolves and prospers in its digital journey. As the guardians of this realm would wisely advise: *"It's not just about the stark figures; it's the stories they whisper that truly matter."*

3.4   Alerts

The unexpected jolt from sleep, the frantic fumbling for the phone, and that stomach-dropping realization that something's amiss. Parents know it all too well, but so do tech professionals. Alerts in the software realm are those distress calls that shake you from your complacency, informing you that your beloved application is not feeling its best. Let's dive into the ins and outs of these digital wake-up calls.

3.4.1   The Essence of Meaningful Alerts

Picture this: your phone buzzes every five minutes, notifying you of trivial matters. Soon, you begin to ignore these pings, assuming they're inconsequential. And then, amidst this cacophony, a crucial alert about a server crash goes unnoticed. This is the trap of redundant alerts.

Example: *A common pitfall many companies face is setting alerts for every minor fluctuation in traffic. While a small drop at 3 am might not be of concern, a massive traffic surge during peak hours surely is. It's all about context and relevance.*

3.4.2   The Art of Channel Prioritization

Just as you'd want an urgent message to be conveyed through the swiftest channel, alerts should also be directed efficiently. Is it a minor glitch that can be addressed in the morning? An email might suffice. Is it a critical server meltdown? Perhaps a loud klaxon or an immediate SMS to the on-call engineer is in order.

Example: *In modern DevOps teams, tools like PagerDuty or Slack integrations can help categorize and route alerts. A database issue might ping the database admin on Slack, while a server failure triggers a phone call to the infrastructure team.*

3.4.3   The Imperative of Regular Testing

Would you trust a fire alarm that hasn't been tested for years? Similarly, an untested alert system is a disaster waiting to happen. Regular checks ensure that when things go south, the alert system won't let you down.

Example: *A famous cloud service provider once faced an issue where their dashboard showed all systems operational, even though a significant outage was underway. It turned out their alerting system, which was supposed to update the dashboard, was also affected. Regular testing might have preemptively identified such dependencies.*

3.4.4   False Positives and The Cry Wolf Syndrome

The tale of the boy who cried wolf isn't just a childhood fable; it's a stark warning against false positives in the world of alerts. When alerts cry havoc without a genuine issue, the risk is twofold: alert fatigue for the team and potential ignorance of genuine problems.

Example: *Imagine an e-commerce platform that sends an alert for every single failed transaction. While a couple of failures might be user errors, a sudden surge in failures could indicate a payment gateway problem. Distinguishing between these scenarios prevents* *unnecessary panic and enables timely interventions.*

In conclusion, keeping a watchful eye on your deployed application ensures that it runs smoothly and efficiently. Remember, it's not paranoia if it's your code child out there! So, channel your inner hawk, equip yourself with the best binoculars, and let's make sure our code kids are always in top form!

4   Summary

In this chapter, we've whimsically navigated the intricate terrains of software deployment. We've likened CI/CD pipelines to "Automating the Scary Stuff," making deployment feel less like a horror movie and more like a well-rehearsed magic trick. Containers have been dubbed "Your Code's Personal Hotel Room," emphasizing the importance of a cozy, tailored environment for code execution. And, of course, we couldn't forget monitoring, our way of "Keeping a Paranoid Eye on Your Code Children," ensuring they play nice and don't wreak havoc. Through various tools and techniques, we've showcased how to refine the deployment process, championing seamless rollouts, and nurturing our code in its ideal habitat.

7

Surviving the Software Development Job

Here, we'll take a heartfelt journey through the ups and downs of being in the vibrant world of software creation. Let's talk about three things every software developer encounters at some point: figuring out what the business really needs, that sneaky feeling of not being good enough (hello, imposter syndrome!), and those moments when it all feels like too much (yep, we're talking burnout). Let's dive in!

1 Understanding Business Requirements: Lost in Translation - Tech Edition

Let's break down the intricate dance of translating business whims into technical wonders into three main acts, each as entertaining as a sitcom episode, yet as serious as your morning coffee.

1.1 The Art of Communication: Tour Guide in Techville

Remember the 'Telephone' game [1] *?* The grown-up version is here, and it's called translating business requirements. Effective communication is the heart of this operation. Picture yourself as a tour guide in the enigmatic land of 'Techville'. *Your group?* Enthusiastic, tech-challenged tourists. *Your mission?* Translate the cryptic dialect of the natives (code) into a language your group can comprehend. It's a bit like watching a foreign film without subtitles, but you're the one providing the live translation. No pressure!

1.2 Deciphering Hieroglyphs: From Business to Binary

Now, the real challenge begins: translating business requirements into technical language. Think of it as being Sherlock Holmes, but instead of solving crimes, you're decoding the business world's enigmas. *Recall the 'coffee ordering app' debacle?* The stakeholder wanted a "simple app to order coffee," and got just black coffee. No lattes, no cappuccinos. *Why?* A classic case of 'Lost in Translation: Tech Edition'. *The lesson?* Dive deep into the subtleties of business language and ask those probing questions. It'll save you from many a facepalm moment.

1.3 Dancing with Stakeholders: The In-Law Tango

Stakeholder collaboration is the third act in our play. Think of it as dealing with in-laws. You might not always get them, but for the

---

[1]   The "Telephone" game, also known as "Chinese Whispers" in some parts of the world, is a popular children's game.

sake of peace (and project success), you've got to tango together. This dance involves managing expectations, brewing many cups of coffee *(or tea, for the refined folks)*, and mastering the art of feedback. A content stakeholder is like a well-fed cat: purring and generous.

In the grand theater of tech, there are countless tales of hits and misses in understanding and translating business requirements. They're not just lessons but also fabulous dinner party stories. So, strap in for the roller coaster that is business requirement translation. With the right moves, it's just another thrilling ride in the tech amusement park.

The Steps of the Tango:

- **Initiation:** Just like the first step in a dance, you need to approach stakeholders with an open mind and a clear understanding of the project's goals. This is where you set the tone for the entire collaboration.
- **Active Listening:** This isn't just about hearing what they say, but truly understanding their needs, concerns, and aspirations. It's the equivalent of following your dance partner's lead.
- **Feedback Loops:** Regular check-ins are crucial. This ensures that you're both on the same page and can adjust your steps as needed. Think of it as the rhythm of the dance.
- **Managing Expectations:** Not every step will be perfect, and not every move will be smooth. It's essential to set realistic expectations from the start and be transparent about any changes or challenges.
- **Closing the Dance:** Once the project is nearing its end, it's time to review, reflect, and ensure that all parties are satisfied with the outcome. Just like a dance, it's essential to finish strong and leave

a lasting impression.

1.3.1 The Role of Empathy

Understanding your stakeholders isn't just about knowing their business requirements. It's about understanding their fears, motivations, and the pressures they face. Just as you'd be considerate of an in-law's feelings and perspectives, the same level of empathy is required here. By putting yourself in their shoes, you can anticipate their needs and address concerns even before they voice them.

1.3.2 Avoiding Missteps

While the tango is a passionate dance, it's also easy to step on your partner's toes if you're not careful. In the world of stakeholder collaboration, these missteps can be misunderstandings, missed deadlines, or misaligned goals. Regular communication, documentation, and a shared vision can help avoid these pitfalls.

In conclusion, dancing with stakeholders is an art that requires patience, understanding, and a willingness to adapt. But with the right approach, it can be a harmonious and rewarding experience for all parties involved.

2 Dealing with Imposter Syndrome: Everybody's Faking It

Imposter syndrome: that insidious, gnawing feeling that you're merely posing as competent while secretly fearing that everyone will uncover your apparent fraudulence. It's like showing up to a fancy costume party only to realize that you're the only one who's actually in a costume. And this is an all-too-common experience in the tech industry, where everyone seems to be running at the speed of light while you feel like you're still trying to put on your running shoes.

2.1 Common Triggers

Common triggers for this confidence-eroding sensation include tackling complex projects, learning new technologies, or merely sharing a meeting room with extremely talented colleagues who seem to invent a new programming language over their coffee breaks.

2.2 A Personal (Fictitious) Anecdote

Allow me to share a somewhat personal *(and by 'personal', I mean completely made up)* story. It all started on my first day at Mega-UltraTechCorp. I was excited, eager, and overwhelmingly terrified. I joined a team working on a bleeding-edge AI project, and my colleagues seemed to have PhDs in everything. And there I was, a humble coder who still needed to Google how to center a div in CSS occasionally.

I remember one meeting when we were discussing the application of quantum computing to improve our AI's predictive capabilities. I nodded along, threw in a thoughtful 'hmm' here and there, but inside, I was screaming: *"When did coding become about understanding quantum mechanics? I'm a fraud! They're going to find out!"*

Then came the day of my first code review. My code was projected onto the wall for everyone to see, like an art critic examining a masterpiece, except this masterpiece was full of bugs. I could almost hear the "Jaws" theme playing in my head. As the team discussed and critiqued my work, I was preparing for my impending unmasking.

2.3   Tackling the Syndrome

But here's the plot twist. It didn't happen. Instead, my team pointed out areas for improvement and also appreciated my fresh perspective. And as I spoke more with my colleagues, I discovered that they also had their own doubts and insecurities. It turns out, we were all feeling like we'd been asked to pilot a spaceship when we'd only just learned to drive.

This revelation was a game-changer. I started managing my imposter syndrome, which let's be real, never really goes away entirely. I began by accepting that it's impossible to know everything, *and that's okay*. I sought mentorship from my more experienced colleagues, celebrated my small victories, and most importantly, voiced my fears and doubts. By normalizing these discussions, we created a supportive environment where everyone could express their vulnerabilities without fear of judgment.

And so, my dear readers, the moral of this fictitious, yet highly relatable story is this: imposter syndrome can hit anyone, anytime. But remember, it's just a syndrome, not a life sentence. With the right strategies, you can manage it, overcome it, and maybe even harness it to push yourself to greater heights. And always remember, in the grand theatre of software development, we're all just improvising.

3 Handling Burnout: Yes, There's Life Beyond the Computer Screen

Let's talk about burnout, a state of chronic exhaustion that can creep up on you like a ninja in the shadows of your professional life. It's the specter that haunts the tech world, often lurking behind the glow of multiple monitors at 2 am. We, developers, face the 'always-on' culture, juggling aggressive deadlines, a constantly evolving tech stack, and the persistent dread of that one bug that refuses to be squashed.

Burnout is not just about being tired. It's a persistent feeling of exhaustion, cynicism, and a sense of reduced efficacy at work. You start viewing your tasks as insurmountable mountains, your code becomes an incomprehensible alien language, and your productivity takes a nose dive. Unchecked, it can lead to health problems, poor job performance, and personal life disruptions.

3.1 The Root Causes

Common causes are often rooted in our work culture and personal habits. Long hours, high workload, feeling a lack of control over your work, or not having your efforts recognized can all fuel this fire. The technology industry is particularly susceptible to this due to its fast-paced and constantly changing nature.

3.2 Strategies for Prevention and Recovery

Preventing and handling burnout requires proactive strategies and a holistic approach.

3.2.1 Establish Work-Life Boundaries

First, draw a clear line between your work and personal life. Just because you can work from anywhere doesn't mean you have to work from everywhere, all the time. Designate 'quiet zones' and 'quiet times' where work can't intrude.

3.2.2 Engage in Non-Technical Hobbies

Second, make sure you're pursuing hobbies and interests outside of coding. Whether it's gardening, rock climbing, knitting, or underwater basket weaving, hobbies provide a refreshing counterbalance to the world of semicolons and curly braces.

3.2.3 Mindfulness and Mental Health

Practicing mindfulness can also be beneficial. Activities like meditation, yoga, or just taking a quiet stroll in nature can help reset your mind and provide much-needed mental peace. Remember, a calm mind is a creative mind. Finally, don't hesitate to seek help if you need it. Talk to your managers, HR, or a mental health professional. Remember, there's no shame in admitting that you're struggling. Everyone needs a helping hand sometimes.

3.3 A Case from the Field: John's Story

To illustrate, let's look at a story from the field. I knew a developer, let's call him John. John was a coding machine, the epitome of the '10x developer'. However, he was also always 'on', working late into the nights and over the weekends. Over time, John's bright spark started to dim. His productivity declined, and he started showing signs of burnout. Recognizing this, John's team intervened. They started by adjusting his workload and ensuring he wasn't working outside of regular hours. John also took up painting, a hobby he had abandoned when his coding career took off. He started meditating and sought professional counseling. Over time, John learned to manage his responsibilities without pushing himself into exhaustion. He found a balance and rekindled his passion for coding.

Remember, there's life beyond the computer screen, and it's crucial for maintaining your life within it. Your mind is like a garden, and just like any garden, it needs care, rest, and variety to thrive. Happy gardening!

4   Summary

In this chapter, we explored the challenges of a software development job, addressing issues such as "Lost in Translation: Tech Edition" when understanding business requirements, coping with "Imposter Syndrome: Everybody's Faking It," and recognizing the importance of "Handling Burnout: Yes, There's Life Beyond the Computer Screen" to maintain a healthy and fulfilling career in the ever-evolving world of software engineering.

8

Collaborative Development: The Anatomy of Teamwork

Just as the human body functions optimally when all its systems and organs work together in harmony, so does the world of software development when its components collaborate seamlessly. Let's delve into the physiology of collaborative development, understanding each system's role in creating a healthy, thriving software project.

1 The Nervous System: Version Control Revisited

If collaborative software development were a living, breathing entity, version control would be its nervous system. Just as our body's neurons transmit messages, version control systems send signals in the form of code changes between various parts of our project. Without it, our body of work might act more like a clumsy toddler than a graceful gymnast, struggling to perform even the simplest of tasks.

1.1 Synaptic Commit Actions: The Power of Atomic Commits

Just as the brain relies on synapses to transmit information efficiently between neurons, atomic commits ensure that each piece of information (or change) in our code is clear and concise. An atomic commit means bundling related changes into a single commit, ensuring that each commit has a unique, self-contained purpose.

Imagine if our synapses fired all over the place without a clear direction. It'd be chaotic! Likewise, grouping unrelated changes in a single commit can lead to confusion for other developers. Keep your commits crisp, like a fresh neuron firing away with purpose.

1.2 Neural Merges: Avoiding the Conflicts

Merge conflicts are the software equivalent of misfired neurons. They occur when there are conflicting changes in different branches that Git cannot reconcile on its own. Properly managing branches and understanding the flow of changes can significantly reduce these "misfires."

Tackling these conflicts is like a neurologist untangling knotted neural pathways. With patience, precision, and a bit of problem-solving, the flow of information can be restored. And if you're the type to often find yourself in the midst of these conflicts, perhaps it's time for a 'neural' checkup – maybe a peer review or two?

1.3 Memory Recall: The Importance of Descriptive Commit Messages

A good commit message is like the brain's ability to recall memories in vivid detail. When we look back through our version control history, a clear commit message tells us exactly what was happening at that point in time.

Ever tried recalling an event from 10 years ago? Now, imagine trying to understand a piece of code from 10 months ago without a clear commit message. It's like trying to remember what you had for lunch three Tuesdays ago without any context. *Was it a sandwich? Sushi? Or perhaps that leftover lasagna?* A concise, descriptive commit message is your roadmap back in time, ensuring that the 'lunches' of your code's past are never forgotten.

2   The Muscular System: Pair Programming

If you've ever been to the gym *(or, more aptly, considered going, browsed fitness videos, then opted for a coding session instead)*, you'll know that muscles are all about coordination. Flex one without the other responding appropriately, and you're in for a world of awkward postures. Enter pair programming: the software development's answer to synchronized muscle movement.

2.1 Synchronous Coding Curls: The Art of Coordination

When you're working in pairs, it's essential that both participants are in sync. One developer, the "driver," actively punches out the code, akin to a bicep contracting for a curl. Meanwhile, the "navigator" reviews the code as it's being written, acting like the tricep, ensuring that the motion remains smooth and balanced. Remember, a single muscle working alone might get a quick result, but it's the combined effort that builds lasting strength. And nobody wants to be that developer with the coding equivalent of skipping leg day!

2.2   Building Robust & Agile Code: The Fitness Regime for Your Software

Just as a coordinated workout can lead to a well-toned physique, pair programming yields robust and agile code [1]. Two heads—or should we say, two muscles—are indeed better than one when spotting those sneaky coding errors. The combined experience and knowledge mean your code gets double the attention, ensuring fewer bugs and more optimal solutions. Think of it as having a personal trainer right beside you, ensuring you don't accidentally drop the weight on your foot... or in this case, the production server.

2.3   Harmonious Development: The Stretching Routine

Every gym enthusiast *(or enthusiastic browser of fitness content)* will preach about the importance of stretching. In pair programming, this translates to ensuring both developers are aligned in their goals and approaches. Communication is the key. Regular check-ins, aligning on coding conventions, and mutual respect are essential to keep

---

[1]   **Agile Code:** Picture a cat in a room full of laser pointers. Every little dot represents a new feature or requirement, and that feline agility is how quickly the cat can pivot, pounce, and chase after each one. Now, imagine that cat's on a caffeine high *(not recommended in reality!)*. That's agile code: effortlessly darting between requirements, adapting on the fly, and always ready for the next unpredictable move. Just remember: while agile code is always on its toes, it's best served with a dash of strategy and not just chasing after every shiny new feature dot!

both 'muscles' limber and in sync. Remember, stretching before jumping into the coding deep end can prevent painful cramps—like those caused by misunderstood requirements or overlooked edge cases.

To cap it off: Just as you wouldn't expect to lift your personal best on your first day at the gym, don't be discouraged if pair programming feels a bit awkward initially. With practice, patience, and a bit of professional banter, your pair programming sessions will become the powerhouse of your software development regime. So, flex those coding muscles and get lifting! *And remember, always be kind to your coding partner; after all, they're the one spotting you.*

3 The Cardiovascular System: Agile Methodologies

Imagine for a moment that your software project is a bustling city. Now, *what's the most important part of that city?* If you're thinking skyscrapers or coffee shops, you might be a caffeine addict like most of us devs. But, in reality, it's the circulatory system: the roads, the subways, the bike lanes. Without these, the city stagnates. Enter Agile Methodologies: the beating heart of the software development world.

3.1 The Agile Heartbeat

The world of Agile methodologies is not unlike the intricate dance of our cardiovascular system. Just as the heart's rhythmic contractions keep us alive and thriving, Agile projects breathe life into the development landscape, each with its distinctive pulse.

3.1.1 Continual Flow of Innovation

Drawing a parallel with the relentless flow of blood, Agile champions a ceaseless stream of innovation. It's not just about getting things done; it's about perpetual advancement. Whether it's a freshly minted feature, a refined line of code, or a user story brought to life, each gets its oxygen-rich burst of attention, ensuring nothing stagnates or gasps for breath.

3.1.2 Every Project's Unique Tempo

Just as every person has a unique heartbeat – from the adrenaline-pumped racer to the serene yogi – every Agile project hums its own tune. Tailored methodologies cater to individual project needs, echoing the diverse landscapes they inhabit. So, when your project seems to whisper, *"I am alive and ready for the next sprint!"*, know that in the developer's dialect, that translates to *"Hey, I haven't encountered an unhandled exception... for now."*

3.2 Scrum vs. Kanban

Let's dive into the vascular system of Agile. Scrum, with its sprints and daily stand-ups, is like the arteries: high pressure, fast-moving, always pushing forward with oxygen-rich ideas. Meanwhile, Kanban, with its continuous flow and emphasis on limits, resembles the veins: steady, calm, and ensuring tasks don't overload the system.

Choosing between Scrum and Kanban is a bit like choosing between cardio and strength training. Both are beneficial; it just depends on what kind of shape you want your project to be in. And let's be real, *who hasn't tried to mix both and ended up with a weird project workout hybrid?*

3.3   Success Stories and Stumbles

Just as our heart rate spikes with excitement or slows during meditation, real-world Agile projects have their peaks and valleys. Some projects race ahead, fueled by espresso shots of innovation, while others may need a little defibrillation *(a.k.a. a quick sprint planning rejig)* to get back on track.

Remember that time the server went down, and everyone's heart rate synced with the refresh button's rhythm? Or that eureka moment during a retrospective when you realized you'd found a more efficient path, sort of like discovering a shortcut in your morning commute? These are the heartbeats of Agile projects: unpredictable, diverse, but always essential to survival.

In conclusion, while you can't wear a fitness tracker to monitor your project's heartbeat *(or can you? Kickstarter idea, anyone?)*, adopting Agile methodologies ensures your software development process remains as fit as a seasoned marathon runner – with possibly just as many coffee breaks!

4   The Digestive System: Code Reviews

We've all heard the saying, "*You are what you eat.*" In the world of software engineering, we might tweak it a bit: "*Your project is what you code.*" Just as the digestive system breaks down our food into usable nutrients and discards the unnecessary bits, code reviews ensure that only the prime, grade-A code makes its way into our projects. Let's chew on this a bit more.

4.1 Preliminary Code Analysis

Diving into a code review without preliminary analysis is like attempting to devour a three-course meal in one bite – ambitious, but not recommended.

4.1.1 The Mouth of the Process

Every grand feast begins with that initial bite, and similarly, every code review starts with an initial analysis - the preliminary examination of the submitted code. Imagine this phase as the mouth of your project's digestive journey. It's not just about passive consumption; it s the first active engagement with what's been served up.

4.1.2 Breaking Down the Code Buffet

In this initial stage, the vastness of raw data - which could range from a few lines to several modules - is divided into digestible fragments. Like how our teeth gnaw, tear, and grind down a mouthful of food, the analysis grinds through lines of code, identifying its structure, main functions, and possible outliers. The aim is to simplify complex portions, turning large chunks into manageable segments that can be more easily processed in the subsequent stages.

4.1.3 Avoiding Preliminary Pitfalls

Venturing into the preliminary analysis is often filled with unforeseen challenges. *Remember the shock of biting into what seemed like a regular piece of chocolate, only to discover a sneaky chili pepper inside?* That's akin to diving into a review and finding hastily written code or overlooked errors. Such moments underscore the importance of approaching this stage with a blend of caution and curiosity. Whether it's a misplaced function, a redundant line, or a logic error, these 'spicy surprises' need early detection to prevent heartburn later in the review process.

4.2   Extracting Beneficial Elements

As the code makes its way down the review pipeline, we reach the metaphorical stomach and intestines of our project. This is where the essential nutrients - the robust functionalities, elegant algorithms, and clean code - get absorbed into the bloodstream of the project. It's all about taking in what will nourish the software and give it strength to perform. Think of it as adding vitamins for vitality and resilience.

4.3   Eliminating Code Waste

The unsung hero of our bodies and, by extension, the part of the code review process that filters out the harmful toxins. This step ensures that bugs, redundancies, or any potential security vulner-abilities are flagged and dealt with. It's the liver's job to ensure that what remains is in the best interest of the body... I mean, the project.

4.4   Navigating Challenges in Code Reviews

Before diving into the main course of code reviews, it's essential to set the table right. Much like ensuring our meals are well-cooked and our utensils are clean, preparing for a code review involves ensuring our codebase is organized and our reviewing tools are set up correctly. But even with the best preparations, there's always room for a few hiccups.

4.4.1 The Spaghetti Scenario

The spaghetti code! The kind where logic is twisted, tangled, and intertwined so intricately, you'd think it came straight out of an Italian kitchen. This dish of a code is not only hard to read but even more challenging to refactor. Just as separating individual spaghetti strands can be a task, untangling such code requires patience, skill, and perhaps a generous sprinkle of code comments for clarity.

4.4.2 Deciphering the Cryptic Comments

We've all been there: staring at a comment in the code and wondering if it's some form of ancient developer hieroglyphics. Whether it's *"This works, but don't ask me how!"* or the ever-mysterious *"TODO: Fix this later,"* these cryptic notes can give even the most seasoned developer indigestion. It's essential to remember that clarity is key, and when in doubt, seeking clarification from the code's author can be a lifesaver.

4.4.3 The Review Remedies

When faced with these challenges, it's not the end of the meal. Every seasoned developer has a toolkit or, in this case, a pantry full of remedies. Adopting a robust set of review guidelines, consistent coding standards, and maintaining open channels of communication can act as the digestive enzymes, breaking down complex issues. Additionally, cultivating a patient mindset, akin to letting a fine wine breathe, allows for a smoother review process, ensuring each line of code gets its moment in the spotlight.

In the grand feast of software development, challenges in code reviews are but a small course. With the right ingredients and a dash of humor, any digestive upset can be transformed into a delightful learning experience.

To sum it up, while we can't offer you a digestive biscuit for your code review sessions, keeping these practices in mind might just make the process a tad more palatable! Cheers to healthy digestion and even healthier code!

5   The Respiratory System: Remote Collaboration

Inhale... Exhale... That's your project taking in fresh insights and expelling outdated practices. Just as our lungs allow us to breathe, remote collaboration brings in a fresh breath of diversity and expertise, nourishing every part of a project.

5.1   Breathing Life from Afar

Collaborative software development isn't confined to the four walls of a traditional office space. The rise of remote collaboration is akin to the deep breaths we take after a brisk walk, necessary and invigorating. With developers collaborating from various corners of the globe:

- **Inhalation (Onboarding):** Like taking in a fresh breath, welcoming remote members is about bringing in diverse perspectives. It's not just about code; it's about varied cultural and experiential inputs that enhance software solutions.
- **Exhalation (Delegation):** Delegating tasks remotely ensures a project's momentum isn't held back. Just as we can't hold our breath for too long without feeling stifled, a project can't hold

onto tasks without passing them to capable hands to keep things moving.

Humorously, there are times when remote collaborations might feel like being "short of breath" – when internet connections fail, or time zones play tricks on synchrony. But, as with any workout, perseverance and routine ensure we develop lung capacity *(or, in our world, efficient collaboration strategies)*.

5.2   Maintaining the Rhythm and Oxygen Balance

Every part of a project requires adequate 'oxygen' (or information) to function. In a distributed setup, it's easy for parts to become 'deoxygenated' or out of the loop. Here's how to ensure an even spread:

- **Regular Check-ins:** Much like our consistent breathing rhythm, regular team check-ins ensure everyone's on the same page. They act as periodic inhalations and exhalations of progress and feedback.
- **Deep Breaths (Focused Sessions):** Sometimes, teams need deeper, more focused breaths. Intensive brainstorming sessions or hackathons act like a lungful of fresh mountain air, reenergizing projects.
- **Avoiding Hyperventilation:** Over-communication can be as detrimental as under-communication. Flooded inboxes and back-to-back virtual meetings can feel like hyperventilating. Balance is key. After all, one wouldn't want to end up in the 'CPR' *(Code Project Resuscitation)* phase, right?

To sum it up, just like our body's need for a balanced respiratory system, software projects require a balanced approach to remote collaboration. It's about ensuring that every part of the project is well-oxygenated with information, insights, and innovations. And remember, it's okay to take deep breaths and pause once in a while; every project needs its moments of reflection and relaxation. So, breathe in, code out!

6 The Immune System: Open Source Contributions

No, I'm not talking about about Moq Library...

Our body's valiant knight against the external invaders. Just as our body beefs up its defenses by recognizing threats and producing specialized antibodies, open source contributions are like the dynamic defenders of the software realm. They bolster, enrich, and shield software, ensuring it remains bug-free and ever-evolving.

6.1 Immunization Through Collaboration

In the body, a vaccine introduces a harmless piece of a virus or bacteria to "train" the immune system to recognize and fight it in the future. In the software world, open source contributions act as these "training drills".

- **Exposure:** By opening up your code to the wider world, you expose it to various coding styles, strategies, and methodologies. It's a bit like letting it play in the mud, and trust me, it builds resilience.
- **Response Mechanism:** When bugs or inefficiencies appear *(and they will)*, the community acts swiftly, producing patches or fixes akin to antibodies. These responses help the software to not

only recover but also to remember and resist similar issues in the future.

Remember the age-old adage? [1] *"It takes a village to raise a child."* Similarly, it often takes a global community to raise a robust piece of software.

6.2   Community-Driven Guard

Software, like our body, isn't immune (pun intended) to occasional sniffles (minor bugs) or even the occasional flu (major vulnerabilities). Community-driven development ensures that:

- **Vigilance is Maintained:** Just as white blood cells patrol our bloodstream, open-source contributors patrol code repositories, always on the lookout for bugs or opportunities to optimize.
- **Rapid Response:** *Got a bug?* There's a good chance that somewhere in the world, someone has faced it, fixed it, and documented it. It's a bit like having an on-call doctor, except this one doesn't charge!

6.3   Celebrating the Antibodies: Open Source Success Stories

Every solution in open source is like an antibody, tailored to combat a specific challenge, and boy, do we have tales of valor to share:

- **Linux:** Starting as a small personal project of Linus Torvalds, it

---

[1]   An "age-old adage" refers to a traditional saying or proverb that has been passed down through generations. "Adage" means a proverb or short statement expressing a general truth. When something is described as "age-old," it emphasizes that it has been recognized or in use for a very long time. So, an "age-old adage" is a traditional, time-tested saying that conveys wisdom or a universal truth.

was the open-source nature of Linux that allowed it to grow into the juggernaut it is today. Talk about a superantibody!

- **Apache HTTP Server:** Like the guardian white cell of the web, the Apache HTTP Server manages and safeguards a significant portion of online domains, thanks to countless contributors who've fortified it over the years.
- **Mozilla Firefox:** *Remember the days when browsing choices were... limited?* Then came Firefox, breathing fresh air and giving users a safer, faster, and more customizable browsing experience. All hail the mighty antibody brigade that keeps refining it!

In conclusion, open source contributions and the immune system share the ethos of collective strength. So the next time you're sneezing from a cold (or a buggy code), remember: there's a vast community of antibodies (contributors) out there, ready to back you up. Bless you! *(For both the sneeze and the code commit).*

7 The Endocrine System: Navigating Team Dynamics

Navigating the world of team dynamics in software development can feel like treading through the intricate network of the endocrine system. Just as hormones play pivotal roles in regulating our moods, energy levels, and overall health, communication and interpersonal relations act as the 'hormones' of a project, influencing its vibe, productivity, and ultimate success.

7.1 Emotional Responses

Have you ever faced a project delay and felt that adrenaline rush, not too dissimilar from the sensation before a bungee jump? Or, on a good day, felt that euphoria of releasing a perfect patch, *akin to a dopamine hit?* That's your team's endocrine system at play, signaling and reacting to various stimuli.

7.2 Communication Disorders

Ineffective communication can lead to what we, in the tech realm, term as "informational hypothyroidism" - sluggish, ineffective, and riddled with misinterpretations. On the flip side, an overload of unnecessary communication feels like an "informational hyperthyroidism" - jittery, overwhelming, and burning everyone out.

7.3 Striking the Balance

However, when the communication is just right, it acts like a well-balanced insulin, ensuring the project's energy (progress) is distributed effectively to all its parts. Regular stand-ups, transparent feedback mechanisms, and recognizing individual contributions can serve as those essential hormones, maintaining the perfect glycemic index for your project's health.

7.4 Monitoring and Interventions

And just as our endocrine system needs periodic checks, monitoring team dynamics is crucial. After all, a sudden spike in 'cortisol' (stress) levels during crunch times might require an 'oxytocin' boost in the form of team-building exercises or appreciation.

In essence, understanding and managing team dynamics is about ensuring the right balance of informational hormones, adjusting doses as per needs, and keeping those metaphorical glands (team members) working in harmony. So the next time you sense some 'hormonal imbalance' in your team, remember - a little endocrinology (communication adjustment) might be all you need. And don't worry, no prescription needed! Just a good ear, an open mind, and maybe a box of chocolates for good measure.

8 Summary

In this chapter, we explored the facets of collaborative software development. We delved into the significance of version control like Git, highlighted the dynamics of pair programming, and discussed the role of Agile frameworks in promoting teamwork and adaptability. The importance of thorough code reviews and the growing relevance of remote collaboration in today's distributed work environment were also addressed. We touched upon the value of open source contributions and navigated the challenges of team dynamics. Overall, the chapter emphasized the tools and methodologies that underpin successful collaborative software projects.

9

Embracing Innovation:
Adventures in Emerging
Technologies

In the ever-evolving world of software engineering, one thing remains consistent: change. With each passing year, we're introduced to technologies that challenge our conventional understanding and push us towards horizons we never thought possible. But as daunting as these changes might sound, they're also immensely exciting! The future, as they say, is written in code—and it's brimming with innovation.

This chapter is your ticket to the forefront of these technological revolutions. From the mind-bending realms of Artificial Intelligence to the tangible networks of IoT, and the virtual wonders of AR/VR

125

to the enigmatic world of Quantum Computing, there's much to uncover. Strap in, dear reader, as we journey through these digital landscapes, laugh at the quirks, and marvel at the possibilities.

1   Exploring AI and Machine Learning: When Code Becomes Intelligent

Ohu, the enigma of Artificial Intelligence and Machine Learning! If you've ever marveled at how Netflix seems to know just the right movie for you or pondered about the chatbot that somehow understands your complex coffee order, then you've already had a brush with these marvels. These technologies are not just shaping our future; they're actively reshaping our present. Let's embark on this journey of understanding and demystifying them.

1.1   The Magic Behind the Screen: AI and ML Defined

Artificial Intelligence (AI) is often mistaken for a robot with a nefarious plan to take over the world. In reality, AI is all about creating machines that can mimic human intelligence processes—though we haven't seen them sip coffee or complain about Mondays... yet. On the other hand, Machine Learning (ML) is a subset of AI, where machines are taught to learn from data without being explicitly programmed. Think of AI as the brain and ML as the ongoing education that brain undergoes.

1.2 Revolution in Digital Landscapes: The AI/ML Impact

From streamlining supply chains to personalizing your movie recommendations, AI and ML are subtly *(and sometimes blatantly)* making their mark. Industries are evolving, software is getting smarter, *and developers?* They're often found in a corner, contemplating if their code will one day code itself.

1.3 Popular Applications: Where AI and ML Shine Bright

While we're still waiting for robots to make a decent espresso, AI and ML have been dazzling us in other domains:

- **Natural Language Processing (NLP):** Why you can chat with a machine and almost forget it doesn't have a pulse.
- **Image Recognition:** Machines recognizing your cat photos before even your friends do.
- **Predictive Analytics:** That uncanny ability of platforms to know you'll buy that taco maker before even you do.

1.4 Data: The Good, The Bad, and The Ethical Dilemmas

In the labyrinth of Artificial Intelligence, if there's one thread that reliably leads us through its complexities, it's data. The stories that numbers tell, the patterns they form, and the insights they reveal are the very lifeblood of our machine counterparts. Just as humans rely on experiences to inform decisions and guide behavior, machines depend on data. However, the sheer volume and nature of this data introduce a host of considerations. Let's journey into the intricate dance between AI and the data it consumes, understanding its potential boons and lurking pitfalls.

1.4.1   The Unquenchable Thirst for Data

Data is to AI what spinach is to Popeye—it fuels it. But unlike our beloved sailor, AI's appetite for data is insatiable. Every click, swipe, like, and share feeds this ever-growing behemoth. And as our digital footprint expands, the corpus of data available for AI systems grows exponentially. With more data, AI models can become more accurate, adaptable, and responsive.

1.4.2   Gold Rush of the Digital Age

The potency of data hasn't gone unnoticed. Companies worldwide are racing to harvest, purchase, or gain access to vast datasets. This fervor for data is reminiscent of the gold rushes of old; with everyone scrambling for a piece of the treasure. But instead of gold pans and shovels, today's prospectors arm themselves with web scrapers and APIs.

1.4.3   The Dark Side of Data

However, with great power comes great responsibility. This relentless pursuit can often overlook crucial aspects such as user consent, data anonymization, and secure storage. *The result?* Potentially invasive breaches of privacy, misuse of personal data, and, yes, algorithms that might inherit and perpetuate biases.

1.4.4   Ethics in the Age of AI

The potential of AI is undeniable, but it's tethered to the quality and integrity of the data it's trained on. Biased data breeds biased algorithms. For instance, if an AI system is primarily trained on images of doctors being male and nurses being female, it might propagate such stereotypes. The stakes are even higher when AI decisions impact areas like criminal justice or loan approvals. It's crucial to address these concerns at the foundational level, ensuring that AI systems are both robust and fair.

1.4.5   A Future We Sculpt

So, while the idea of a robot uprising remains in the realm of science fiction (for now), the ethical dilemmas surrounding data and AI are very much a reality. As we stand on the precipice of a new era, it's imperative to shape the future of AI with intentionality, ethical rigor, and a deep understanding of the potential consequences.

1.5   AI/ML in Software Engineering: Changing the Game

While some software engineers fear AI might steal their jobs, the savvy ones know that it's more about *collaboration than competition*. Automated testing powered by AI ensures you catch that pesky bug before it reaches your users. Code generation via ML can reduce manual grunt work. *Remember, a smart developer uses AI; a smarter one knows its strengths and limitations.*

2   Diving into IoT: When Your Fridge Talks to Your Thermostat

We've always yearned for our gadgets to be a bit smarter. Little did we know they'd start forming their own social network! Welcome to the world of the Internet of Things (IoT), where devices chat about everything from your milk's expiry date to the optimal room temperature. Let's dive into this interconnected realm.

2.1   The Great Device Social Network: Defining IoT

Imagine for a moment a world where your coffee maker knew your alarm clock's ringtone and started brewing just as you hit the snooze button. *Sounds magical, doesn't it?* That's the premise of the Internet of Things (IoT). At its core, IoT connects everyday devices to the internet, allowing them to send, receive, and process data. It's like Facebook for gadgets, minus the status updates (thankfully).

The breadth of IoT's realm is vast. Consider smart thermostats that intelligently adjust room temperatures based on your daily patterns, optimizing comfort and conserving energy. Then, there are wearable fitness trackers that monitor your physical activity, sleep quality, and other health metrics, providing insights and nudging you towards healthier habits.

In urban settings, we're seeing the rise of smart infrastructure. Picture a city where traffic light timings are adjusted in real-time based on the flow of vehicles, significantly reducing traffic congestion. For the agriculturally inclined, imagine farms where sensors embedded in the ground detect moisture levels and trigger automated irrigation systems. This ensures crops receive just the right amount of water, optimizing yield while conserving resources.

Home automation is another domain where IoT shines. There are doorbells equipped with cameras and speakers, allowing homeowners to see and communicate with visitors remotely. Light bulbs, blinds, and even kitchen appliances can be controlled through a centralized system or smartphone application.

On an industrial level, machinery equipped with myriad sensors can forecast potential breakdowns. By analyzing patterns and detecting anomalies, these systems can predict when maintenance is due, effectively reducing downtimes and maximizing productivity.

2.2 From Smart Toasters to Industrial Titans: The Spectrum of IoT

Once upon a time, the term 'smart device' was exclusive territory for our beloved phones. Today, this prestigious label has been adopted by an array of devices, from the benign toaster warming our breakfast to the complex sensors guiding massive industrial machines.

At home, we're experiencing a subtle revolution. Lightbulbs adjust according to our moods, thermostats learn our preferred temperatures, and refrigerators might soon chide us for that extra slice of cake. These devices, though seemingly trivial, are shaping a more responsive living environment, attuned to our habits and needs.

But stepping out of our homes, the scale and stakes of IoT amplify. In industries, we're not just talking about efficiency; we're discussing precision, safety, and productivity. Sensors in factories monitor equipment health, ensuring timely maintenance to prevent costly downtimes. In agriculture, drones fly overhead, scanning fields to provide insights for better crop yield. And in the vast world of logistics, IoT aids in tracking, ensuring that our packages, whether a cherished gift or crucial medicine, reach us on time.

For software engineers navigating this IoT spectrum, the journey is both exhilarating and daunting. The coding strategies, data management techniques, and security protocols that work for a smart mirror might not hold water in an industrial setting. With the proliferation of devices, there's the ever-present challenge of interoperability, ensuring that the smart door lock can communicate seamlessly with the smart security camera.

And hovering above all these technicalities is the omnipresent cloud of data security. While a data breach from your smart blender revealing your smoothie preferences might raise a chuckle, leaks from more critical devices can have serious implications.

2.3 Building Bridges: Software in the IoT Age

Software development for IoT is akin to constructing a grand linguistic translator, catering to a cacophony of device dialects. Here's a more detailed exploration of what this entails:

- **Diverse Device Landscape:** The world of IoT isn't restricted to just smart thermostats or fitness trackers. It ranges from simple sensors in agricultural fields to sophisticated machinery in factories. Each of these devices has its unique specifications, data formats, and communication protocols. Crafting software that caters to this broad spectrum demands flexibility and adaptability.
- **Integration and Interoperability:** It's one thing to develop software for a singular device; it's another to ensure that multiple devices can communicate smoothly. For instance, in a smart home, you might want the lights to dim as soon as the home theater system starts playing a movie. This seamless interaction requires intricate integrations, translating one device's "language" into another's.
- **Real-time Processing:** Many IoT applications demand real-time responses. Picture a health monitor that tracks a patient's vitals. If something goes awry, the system needs to alert medical personnel

instantaneously. Building software that can process data and react in real-time is no small feat.

- **Security and Privacy:** As the number of connected devices balloons, so does the potential attack surface for malicious entities. Ensuring that data transmissions are secure, access controls are robust, and personal information remains confidential is paramount. It's not just about avoiding glitches; it's about safeguarding user trust.
- **Scalability:** Today, a city might deploy a few hundred traffic sensors. Tomorrow, they might want to scale it to thousands. Software solutions need to be designed with scalability in mind, ensuring that as the number of devices grows, performance doesn't take a nosedive.
- **Reliability and Redundancy:** High stakes are involved, especially when considering applications like smart vehicles. While a bug in a gaming app might lead to user frustration, a glitch in a vehicle's brake system can be catastrophic. Software for such applications not only needs rigorous testing but also built-in redundancy to handle unexpected scenarios.

Software development in the IoT realm is both a challenge and an adventure. As developers, it's our task to weave the digital threads that allow these devices to harmonize in the vast orchestra of interconnected technology.

2.4 Security, Privacy, and the Inevitable Headaches

Embracing the interconnected world of IoT is akin to opening Pandora's Box. Sure, the marvels inside are astounding — everything's interconnected, your smartwatch chats with your coffee machine, your car sends reminders to your phone about refueling. But in this symphony of communication, there's a silent player lurking: the question of security and privacy.

The more devices we connect, the more doors we inadvertently open for potential intruders. Data breaches aren't just about compromised credit card details anymore; it's about unauthorized access to personal habits, preferences, and routines. And let's face it: in a world where data is the new gold, your smart fridge knowing you're a midnight snacker becomes more than a personal quirk — it's valuable information.

To navigate this digital minefield, software engineers and developers need more than just coding finesse. They need an in-depth understanding of potential vulnerabilities, continuously evolving security protocols, and a proactive approach to potential threats. Consider this: your smartphone gets periodic security updates, *right?* Now imagine extending that protective umbrella to every single connected device in your ecosystem, from the thermostat on your wall to the fitness tracker on your wrist.

2.5   The IoT in Action

The marvels of IoT aren't hidden in arcane journals or locked behind laboratory doors; they are part and parcel of our everyday life. Those wristbands that track your heart rate? That's IoT at work. The smart irrigation systems ensuring plants get just the right amount of water based on weather forecasts? A nod to IoT again.

In the realm of software engineering, this tech wonder has given birth to applications that felt like science fiction just a decade ago. We're talking about software that allows factory managers to monitor equipment health in real-time from the other side of the planet or systems predicting when a machine will break down, well before it even coughs.

But if you think that's the peak of IoT's potential, think again. Rumor has it, in a lab nestled deep in Silicon Valley *(or perhaps in someone's backyard garage)*, there's a prototype of a 'Smart Sofa' – it not only adjusts its cushion firmness based on your mood but also orders pizza for you when it detects you've had a bad day. Now, if only it could also console you about your favorite show's season finale!

In this digital age, as IoT continues to permeate every facet of our lives, it's not just about connectivity, but how these connections make our lives not only more efficient but also a tad more whimsical.

3   AR and VR

The realms of Augmented Reality (AR) and Virtual Reality (VR) are no longer reserved for sci-fi novels or futuristic fantasies. They have woven their way into our daily lives, blurring the lines between the tangible and the virtual. Whether you're conjuring up digital overlays in a city street or diving deep into an entirely virtual universe, AR and VR technologies are redefining the way we interact with the world and, more interestingly, how we define reality itself.

3.1   The Magic of AR and VR

Picture this: You're wandering the streets of ancient Rome, marveling at the architectural genius of the Colosseum, and then suddenly, you're defending your spaceship from alien invaders. A moment later, you're back on your living room couch, headset in hand. Welcome to the world of Augmented Reality (AR) and Virtual Reality

(VR). AR adds a sprinkle of digital magic to our real world, overlaying graphics, sounds, and tactile feedback onto our surroundings. Imagine looking at a restaurant and instantly seeing its menu, reviews, and a floating arrow pointing you to the closest parking spot—talk about a seamless blend of the digital and physical realms! On the other hand, VR immerses you entirely into a computer-generated environment. It's so immersive, you might just try reaching out for a virtual donut *(but alas, it's calorie-free and not as tasty).*

3.2 Crafting AR and VR Experiences

Software engineering for AR and VR isn't just about lines of code; it's about crafting experiences. This realm demands engineers to not only be adept with sophisticated tools and frameworks but also to possess a dash of imagination. Think about it. Crafting a VR game is more than just ensuring the physics is right; it's about ensuring that the user feels the weight of that enchanted sword they're swinging. Or in an AR application for architects, it's about making sure that the digital overlay of a building structure aligns flawlessly with the real-world terrain. But be wary: you might create a VR experience so engaging that users might prefer their virtual pets over their real-world, slightly jealous cats. *Who knew coding could lead to feline feuds?*

As the line between the digital and physical continues to blur, AR and VR stand at the forefront, offering limitless potential. From revolutionizing how we play and learn to transforming industries like healthcare and real estate, they're reshaping our reality — one pixel at a time.

4 Quantum Computing

The digital realm has long been governed by the zeros and ones of binary bits. But what if we told you there's a computational realm where bits could be both zero and one simultaneously? Welcome to the world of quantum computing, where the rules of classical physics take a back seat, and things get a wee bit... spooky. Let's dive into this quantum rabbit hole but beware; things might get a little... entangled.

4.1 Qubits and Quantum Gates

While our good old bits come in two flavors —zeros and ones— qubits (quantum bits) prefer to have their cake and eat it too. Unlike classical bits, qubits can exist in a superposition of states, which means they can represent both zero and one simultaneously. And, if that wasn't wild enough, qubits can also become 'entangled,' wherein the state of one qubit can instantly influence the state of another, regardless of distance. Talk about a cosmic relationship! Now, with quantum gates, which are the quantum counterparts to classical logic gates, we can manipulate these qubits to perform computations. *Imagine trying to explain that at a dinner party without everyone thinking you've had a bit too much to drink.*

4.2 Quantum Potential

Quantum computing is like your regular computing but on some serious computational steroids. Its ability to process vast amounts of information simultaneously gives it an edge in solving problems classical computers might find, well, a tad challenging. From cryptography, where it promises to both secure data and break codes, to optimization problems where finding the best solution is akin to searching for a needle in a cosmic haystack, quantum computing is paving the way. And for software engineers, this means mastering new algorithms and techniques. Like using Shor's algorithm, which could one day make our current encryption look as sturdy as a paper lock.

4.3 Quantum Quirks and Conundrums

Now, before you toss away your trusty classical computer, it's worth noting that quantum computing is still in its infancy. While the potential is monumental, so are the challenges. Maintaining the delicate quantum state of qubits is no easy task; they're sensitive little things that can be disturbed by the slightest environmental changes. Plus, there's the issue of error rates and ensuring that quantum computations are reliable. It's like trying to write a novel on a typewriter that occasionally types in Klingon. While we're making strides in improving quantum tech, it's safe to say that our classical computers won't be joining the dodo bird anytime soon.

In the ever-evolving world of software engineering, quantum computing stands as a testament to our unyielding quest to push boundaries. It's a thrilling, albeit complex, frontier that beckons engineers to explore, innovate, and, occasionally, scratch their heads in sheer quantum befuddlement.

5 Summary

In this chapter, we delved deep into the frontier of emerging technologies, beginning with the cerebral realms of AI and ML and their transformative effects on industries and software development. We ventured into the interconnected world of IoT, where even the most mundane objects become part of a grand digital symphony. Our journey took a visual turn with AR and VR, where digital and physical realities blend seamlessly. Finally, we touched the quantum realm, challenging our conventional understanding of computation. Through each section, the underlying message was clear: the future of software engineering is vibrant, multi-dimensional, and brimming with potential. As we navigate this ever-evolving landscape, it is imperative to marry innovation with responsibility, ensuring our creations benefit society as a whole.

10

Future-Proofing Yourself in
the World of Software

Welcome to Chapter 10! Think of this as your personal tour through the fascinating world of software. You might have heard that it's all about ones and zeros, but there's so much more to it. *Isn't it funny?* In a realm filled with logic and code, it's often us unpredictable humans that throw in the biggest curveballs. Let's dive in and uncover the wonders together!

1   Every Day is a School Day

In the world of software engineering, the only thing that's certain is the fact that you'll probably be outdated tomorrow – and no, we're not just talking about the stylish, retro 90s t-shirt you love wearing to code sprints.

1.1   The Relentless Pace of Software Evolution

Technology progresses at a breakneck speed, and with it, the tools, languages, and methodologies we rely upon. To stay relevant as a software engineer is to engage in a never-ending dance of learning. It's like being back in school, minus the awkward teenage years *(or for some of us, with the awkwardness still firmly intact)*.

Consider this: A decade ago, could you have predicted the dominance of containerization, the rise of functional programming in mainstream software development, or *how Machine Learning would creep into seemingly every application?* This unpredictability is both a challenge and an excitement of the profession.

1.2   Sharpening the Saw: Tools and Tricks to Stay Updated

So how does one avoid becoming a 'software dinosaur'? For starters, drop the "*I've always done it this way*" mindset. Your first web page might have been built with blinking marquees and spinning GIFs, but it's time to move on!

- **Conferences & Workshops:** They aren't just for collecting cool swag. They offer valuable insights into upcoming trends and hands-on experiences. Plus, the networking! Who knows, you might just meet someone who's been wrestling with the same bug as you.
- **Online Courses & Tutorials:** Platforms like Coursera, Udacity, and Pluralsight are packed with up-to-date content. They're the Netflix for techies, but instead of binge-watching, you're binge-

learning!

- **Forums & Online Communities:** Engage in places like Stack-Overflow, GitHub, or Reddit's r/programming. Get feedback, share solutions, and enjoy that random humorous comment that makes your day.
- **Tech Blogs & Newsletters:** Keeping up with industry news is essential. Subscribe to leading tech publications, and maybe even start your own blog. Documenting your learning journey helps solidify concepts and, hey, showing off a bit doesn't hurt.
- **Open Source Contribution:** Not only does it feel good to give back, but it's also a prime way to learn. Dive into different projects and see how the magic happens behind the scenes.
- **Work at eBiz consulting GmbH:** *(Added with a wink because, full disclosure, that's where I work!)*: For those in the know, eBiz is the unofficial academy for the modern developer. But don't rush to send in your resumes just yet; this isn't a paid ad. It's more of a cheeky nod from yours truly, who might be just a tad biased. [1]

Remember, the aim isn't to know everything *(leave that to omniscient beings and search engines)*, but to remain curious and adaptable. As the old saying goes, "The day you stop learning is the day you become obsolete" - or *was that just a pop-up warning on an old software installer?* Either way, it holds true.

---

[1]   In all seriousness, while eBiz is fantastic *(in this writer's humble and totally unbiased opinion)*, the journey of continuous learning is multifaceted and not confined to one's workplace. But if you ever find yourself there, say hi and share a joke about the old times!

2 Soft Skills in a Hard-Coded World

In the binary world of 1s and 0s, it's easy to forget there's a whole spectrum of skills that don't revolve around your keyboard. While algorithms and data structures form the backbone of software development, soft skills are its lifeblood, enabling projects to flow smoothly, teams to collaborate seamlessly, and innovations to be communicated effectively. Sure, your code might be the star of the show, but soft skills are the director, scriptwriter, and occasionally, the crisis manager when the lead actor forgets their lines *(because, you know, bugs happen)*. Let's take a closer look at why soft skills are your unsung heroes in the programming saga.

2.1 Talk the Talk, Don't Just Code the Code

Despite common misconceptions and a slew of 90's hacker movies, developers aren't solely keyboard sorcerers whispering arcane incantations in Python, JavaScript, or the melodious songs of C#. *(Because let's face it, sometimes we all need a little sharp note in our code.)* In the modern age, developers have a dual role. Sure, they're code composers, but they also need to translate their tech symphonies for the uninitiated. What good is a magnum opus in C# if you can't convey its majesty to non-tech folks or (gasp!) endure a team meeting without summoning the ghost of deprecated methods?

Empathy and articulate communication aren't just luxuries; they're essentials. They bridge the chasm between *"It's done when it's done"* and *"Here's why we're taking this approach."* Plus, they're the trusty sidekicks in preventing those awkward moments when the client stares blankly and says, *"I thought 'object-oriented' meant it was user-friendly."*

2.2   Navigating the Complex Waters of Team Dynamics

If coding was a video game, teamwork would be that tricky level many developers get stuck on. But let's be honest, in the multiplayer game of software development, you want the best squad on your side. This means appreciating diverse perspectives, sharing the keyboard from time to time, and realizing that a code review isn't a personal affront, but a chance to level-up.

Handling conflicts is part and parcel of the journey. Remember, it's not about whose code reigns supreme *(though, of course, yours is pretty darn good)*, but what solution best fits the quest at hand. When tensions run high, take a deep breath, sip that cold coffee *(because you forgot about it... again)*, and approach the situation with an open mind.

2.3   Beyond the Code: Working with the Muggles

Let's face it, there will come a time (probably several) when you'll need to work with folks who think 'Java' is just an exotic type of coffee. These interactions can be gold mines of opportunity if navigated correctly. Presentations to non-tech teams are not a chance to show off your encyclopedic knowledge of esoteric algorithms, but to bridge the gap between tech and business. The goal? Make them understand and value your hard work—without the jargon.

Just remember: *While it may seem like you're speaking different languages, you're all working towards a common goal. And if all else fails, a well-timed tech joke can break the ice: "Why did the* *developer go broke? Because he used up all his cache."*

Soft skills, though often overlooked in the echo chambers of code repositories, can make or break your career. So, while you sharpen your coding skills, don't forget to polish that emotional intelligence of yours. It's the secret sauce that complements the code, turning good developers into great ones.

3   Specialization vs. Generalization

In the ever-fluctuating realm of software engineering, one dilemma persists through the ages, causing many a sleepless night *(apart from that elusive bug, of course)*: to specialize or to generalize? It's akin to choosing between a Swiss army knife and a master-crafted katana. Each has its charm, its strength, and its own set of whimsical jokes attached to it.

Let's break it down:

Specialization: The Deep Dive Approach

Specialists are the individuals who've chosen a niche and are de-termined to become the Gandalfs of that domain, uttering, "*You shall not pass*" to any problem that dares come their way. Whether it's cloud computing, blockchain, or the dark arts of optimizing C++ com-pilers, these folks have dived deep. The advantages? High demand in their chosen niche and the ability to command a premium for their in-depth expertise. The downside? Well, niches can change or, in the worst-case scenario, disappear. Remember Flash developers? Precisely.

Generalization: The Panoramic View

On the flip side, we have the generalists. These are the Swiss army knives of the tech world, always equipped with a tool for every situation, even if it's just the tech equivalent of a toothpick. By having a broad understanding of various domains, they can weave between roles, adapt to different teams, and, most importantly, see connections that specialists might miss. Their challenge? Standing out in a vast sea and ensuring they don't spread themselves too thin, becoming, well, *the jack of all trades and master of none.*

The Million-Dollar Question: Which Path to Choose?

For those at the crossroads, it might feel like being asked to choose their favorite programming language *(though, come on, we all know it's whichever one is causing the least Kopfschmerzen* [1] *at the moment)*. It boils down to individual preference and market demand. *Passionate about a particular domain?* Dive in! *Prefer varied challenges and wearing multiple hats?* Broaden that horizon!

It's also worth noting that in this digital era, many find themselves in a 'T-shaped' model—having broad knowledge in multiple areas but diving deep into one or two specialties. Think of it as having your cake and eating it too, but with occasional crumbs of impostor syndrome.

In conclusion, whether you're gearing up to be the tech world's Gandalf or its MacGyver, remember that both paths come with their own set of adventures. It's less about which path is 'better' and more about which journey you want to embark on.

---

[1]   Ohoo your german is getting better! Yes, it means 'headaches'.

4 With Great Code, Comes Great Responsibility

As developers, we know that with every line of code we write, we're weaving the very fabric of a digital society. And, much like Spider-Man with his web, it's essential to ensure our digital threads don't inadvertently tangle anyone up—or worse. Ethics in software is more than just ensuring you don't "borrow" a chunk of code from StackOverflow without understanding it. It's the north star that should guide each algorithm, each app, and every frustrated desk flip.

4.1 Data Privacy: More Than Just a Checkbox

In an era where your fridge can tweet and teapots might just spill more than just tea, data privacy is paramount. It's no longer just about not storing passwords as plain text *(which, if you're doing, please pause reading this and go fix that, we'll wait)*. It's about understanding and respecting the immense trust users place in us with their data. Sure, GDPR might seem like that party guest who's overstayed their welcome, but its principles are crucial. After all, just because you can know how often someone opens their fridge at midnight, doesn't mean you should.

4.2 Societal Impact of Emerging Tech

AI, AR, VR, IoT... the tech world does love its abbreviations. But behind each catchy acronym lies a power that can transform societies—for better or for worse. As developers, it's our job to ensure our innovations uplift rather than oppress. *Building a facial recognition system?* Consider its implications and potential misuse. *Creating a deepfake generator?* Ponder the ethical ramifications. And if you're making a toaster that learns users' toast preferences and tries to engage in morning banter? Well, just remember that no one likes a sassy appliance before their first coffee.

Ethics in software engineering isn't just a philosophical discussion reserved for tech conferences or late-night debates over cold pizza. It's a lived experience, a daily commitment, and a reminder that with every function and feature, we're impacting lives. So, let's make sure it's for the right reasons and not just because we can. Because, in the immortal words of many a developer: "It seemed like a good idea at the time" is a sentiment best left for questionable fashion choices, not code.

5   The Circle of Code

The circle of code is like the circle of life, but with fewer lions and more lines of logic. Every seasoned developer remembers starting out with a blank slate—or rather, a blank IDE—in the vast savannah of software engineering. Just as Simba had Mufasa to guide him *(at least for a while)*, every coder can benefit from a guiding hand. Mentorship plays a pivotal role in the growth and development of young devs.

Every developer knows the struggle—the countless hours deciphering an error message more cryptic than ancient hieroglyphics or realizing a misplaced semicolon caused utter chaos. As these moments contribute to our battle scars *(and perhaps a few gray hairs)*, there's an opportunity to save someone else from these pitfalls. By mentoring newer developers, not only do you help them sidestep common obstacles, but you also invest in building a more robust community. After all, today's junior devs are tomorrow's tech leads.

In the expansive world of open source and vast online communities, the spirit of sharing is alive and well. And no, we're not talking about that one time you hoarded your coveted debugging trick. Contributing to the community isn't just about personal acclaim; it's about nurturing an ecosystem where ideas flourish. Whether sharing insights on a forum, contributing to an open-source project, or imparting wisdom about the latest C# quirks, every bit helps keep the circle going.

Beyond the warm and fuzzy feelings, there's a tangible upside to giving back. Teaching is one of the best ways to learn. Guiding others often shines a light on gaps in your understanding, and being surrounded by curious minds keeps you agile. Their fresh perspectives can prompt innovative solutions you hadn't previously considered. So, in the software development jungle, where adaptability reigns supreme *(or was it the lion?)*, be ready to both teach and learn.

6   The Only Constant in Tech is Change

In an industry where every software release feels like a fast-forward button, the tides of technology are more unpredictable than a caffeinated programmer without access to coffee. The codebase that was your Bible today might very well become an ancient relic by tomorrow. But here's the kicker: it's not about the waves; it's about how well you surf.

(1) **Shift Your Mindset:** Embrace the reality that the stability you seek in tech is a myth, akin to the fabled "bug-free code" or the mysterious full-stack unicorn. Instead of viewing change as a disruptor, see it as an invitation—a ticket to the front row seat

of innovation. By fostering a mindset that thrives on adaptability, you not only survive but thrive amidst the frenetic pace of change.

(2) **Stay Curious:** Remember the time you first got your hands on a piece of code and felt like a wizard casting spells? Hold onto that child-like wonder. Stay curious. Dive deep into new libraries, frameworks, and languages. It's a big tech world out there, and the more you explore, the more you'll be prepared for its twists and turns.

(3) **Hone Your Skills in the "Art of Letting Go":** Developers, brace yourselves. Not all your code will make it to the Hall of Fame. Some of it might become obsolete faster than you can say "deprecated." The art lies in discerning when to hold onto older technologies and when to move on. It's the tech equivalent of decluttering your wardrobe; if you haven't used it in a year, maybe it's time to say goodbye.

(4) **Holistic Development:** Beyond the code, invest in your personal growth. Whether it's mindfulness practices to stay grounded amidst tech turbulence or networking to keep a pulse on industry shifts, your personal development is the anchor in this ever-evolving tide.

(5) **Life Beyond the IDE:** While you're battling bugs or architecting the next big thing, don't forget to step outside your Integrated Development Environment (IDE). Tech changes, but life's constants—like sunsets, friendships, and the joy of a well-cooked meal—remain. Embrace experiences outside the tech bubble. They provide perspective, balance, and often the inspiration for your next big idea.

(6) **Develop a Habit of Reflective Practice:** Set aside time for reflection. Whether it's a weekly review or an annual personal

retrospective, look back at where you've been, what you've learned, and chart out where you want to go. In a sea of rapid iterations, your reflective practice is the compass you didn't know you needed.

To sum up, in the world of software, the only guarantee we have is that of change. But with the right perspective and a toolkit of resilience strategies, we can navigate these changes not with trepidation but with gusto. After all, every new tech wave is just another opportunity to redefine the status quo, ride the edge of innovation, and maybe —just maybe— leave behind a legacy that survives at least a couple of software releases.

7   Summary

In this chapter, we've delved into the importance of continuous learning in the ever-evolving software landscape, emphasizing that every day truly is a school day for the dedicated developer. We explored the critical role of soft skills, underscoring the fact that coding is but half the battle; effective communication, teamwork, and empathy remain vital ingredients for success. The debate between specialization and generalization was presented, highlighting the nuanced decisions developers face in carving their unique paths. Ethical considerations took center stage as we grappled with the weighty responsibilities that come with our coding powers. We touched upon the significance of mentorship and the enriching cycle of giving back, and finally, navigated the inherent uncertainties of the tech world, reinforcing that adaptability is key. This chapter sought to complement the technical intricacies of software engineering with a broader, holistic view, emphasizing personal growth and the wider implications of our roles in the industry.

Let's Say Goodbye

Dear reader [1], we've reached the final chapter – the moment when we bid adieu, like old friends parting ways after a fantastic journey. But don't worry, I promise this isn't a "goodbye forever," it's more like a "see you later." After all, the world of software engineering is a dynamic one, and who knows, we might meet again in the realm of code, bugs, and endless debugging sessions.

As we wrap up our tech-infused adventure, let's take a moment to reflect. We've journeyed through the ups and downs of the software development life cycle, deciphered the art of coding, dabbled in the mysterious world of version control, and even survived the chaos monkeys of software testing. We've transformed into software archaeologists, unraveling legacy code's ancient secrets, and embraced the ever-changing landscapes of deployment, all while learning to thrive in the world of tech.

I hope this book has been your trusty guide, your virtual mentor, and your companion in unraveling the mysteries of software engineering. If you've had a laugh or two along the way, even better! After all,

---

[1]   You.

153

humor is like a secret sauce that makes learning a tad bit more exciting and memorable.

As you venture forth, armed with newfound knowledge and a toolkit full of tech tricks, remember that the software world is your canvas. Embrace innovation, be curious, and never shy away from challenges. And if you ever find yourself in a coding conundrum, just think back to the times when software development felt like playing 20 questions with stakeholders – you've got this!

So, until our paths cross again, keep coding, keep creating, and keep that love-hate relationship with software engineering alive. Who knows, maybe next time we meet, *you'll be the one writing a book*, sharing your tech adventures and sprinkling a little humor along the way.

Until then, happy coding, my fellow tech enthusiast. May your bugs be minor, your code be elegant, and your journey be as rewarding as compiling code without errors on the very first try.

Farewell for now, and – *keep the debugger close, and your sense of humor even closer!*

Yours in code and laughter,

Mabrouk Mahdhi [1]

---

[1]   The author of this book.

A

About the Author

Mabrouk Mahdhi is a Senior Technical Consultant at *eBiz Consulting GmbH*. With an impressive track record of successfully handling complex projects for well-known automobile manufacturers and an industrial gas company in Germany, and with over *11 years of industrial experience*, Mabrouk has demonstrated his expertise in navigating the intricacies of software development with finesse. His invaluable experience and passion for technology shine through in the pages of this book, as he skillfully weaves together his knowledge and humor to take readers on a delightful journey through the world of software engineering.

B

The Voice Behind the Foreword

André Dammeyer is a software architect and founder of eBiz Consulting GmbH, a digital solutions company. He has led many software projects for various companies, using both on-premises and cloud technologies. He has more than 20 years of experience in software development and architecture. He is an expert in software integration and scalability. His knowledge and skills make him a sought-after expert.

C

Abbreviations

A

- **API**: Application Programming Interface

C

- **CDN**: Content Delivery Network
- **CI/CD**: Continuous Integration/Continuous Deployment
- **C#**: C-Sharp (Programming Language)

G

- **GDPR**: General Data Protection Regulation

H

- **HTML**: Hypertext Markup Language
- **HTTPS**: Hypertext Transfer Protocol Secure

I

- **IDE**: Integrated Development Environment

J

- **JSON**: JavaScript Object Notation
- **JVM**: Java Virtual Machine
- **Jenga**: A popular block-stacking game

M

- **MVC**: Model-View-Controller

O

- **OOP**: Object-Oriented Programming

S

- **SDLC**: Software Development Life Cycle
- **SQL**: Structured Query Language

U

- **UI**: User Interface
- **URL**: Uniform Resource Locator

X

- **XSS**: Cross-Site Scripting